OF SOUND MIND TO MARRY

OF SOUND MIND TO MARRY

A REALITY CHECK FROM THE MARRIAGE COUNSELOR FOR PRE-WEDS

Jim Bierman

Westport, Connecticut
London

Library of Congress Cataloging-in-Publication Data

Bierman, Jim, 1954–
Of sound mind to marry : a reality check from the marriage counselor
for pre-weds / Jim Bierman.
   p. cm.
  Includes bibliographical references and index.
  ISBN 978–0–313–34723–8 (alk. paper)
  1. Marriage counseling. 2. Marriage. 3. Couples. I. Title.
  HQ10.B54 2008
646.7′7—dc22   2007029030

British Library Cataloguing in Publication Data is available.

Library of Congress Catalog Card Number: 2007029030
ISBN: 978–0–313–34723–8

First published in 2008

Praeger Publishers, 88 Post Road West, Westport, CT 06881
An imprint of Greenwood Publishing Group, Inc.
www.praeger.com

Printed in the United States of America

The paper used in this book complies with the
Permanent Paper Standard issued by the National
Information Standards Organization (Z39.48–1984).

10 9 8 7 6 5 4 3 2 1

Copyright Acknowledgments

MATCHMAKER from the Musical FIDDLER ON THE ROOF
SUNRISE, SUNSET from the Musical FIDDLER ON THE ROOF
Words by Sheldon Harnick, Music by Jerry Bock. Copyright © 1964 (Renewed
1992) Mayerling Productions Ltd. (Administered by R&H Music) and Jerry Bock
Enterprises for the United States and Alley Music Corporation, Trio Music
Company, and to Jerry Bock Enterprises for the world outside of the United States.
Used by permission. All rights reserved.

Excerpt from "West-Running Brook" from THE POETRY OF ROBERT FROST
Copyright 1928, 1969 by Henry Holt and Company. Copyright 1956 by Robert
Frost. Reprinted by permission of Henry Holt and Company, LLC.

We can't do ourselves justice by letting our tribute end in the wedding ceremony. You have to move from ceremony to sacrament. Sacrament takes up where ceremony leaves off. Ceremony is like putting a ring on her finger at the wedding, but sacrament is ringing her life with love and joy every day and every hour.

—Rev. Joseph Lowery, paraphrased from his dedication to Rosa Parks, November 2, 2005

Contents

- Psychological Assessment
  PREPARE/ENRICH
  16PF® Couple's Counseling Questionnaire
  Taylor-Johnson Temperament Analysis® (T-JTA®)
  PREP-M
- Focus for Continued Professional Development

Acknowledgments

I started writing this book to add more of a reasoning influence to those who are madly in love and planning to marry. I believe in love and marriage and wish above all else to help others make love last. I remember Wendell Berry's beautiful poem "The Country of Marriage" in which he said:

> How many times have I come into you out of my head with joy,
> for to approach you, I have given up all light and all directions.
> I come to you lost, wholly trusting, like a man walking into a forest
>   unarmed...
> I rest in peace in you when I arrive at last...
> ...and this poem (is) no more mine than any man's who has loved a
>   woman.

I believe that we can enter into this forest of love armed with the wisdom of our culture and not sacrifice love's passion in the process. I believe we can be wholly trusting of each other and ourselves without feeling lost; when we are well-informed about the many faces of love, we can surrender to passion with confidence because we know ourselves and our loved one. We can arrive at that peaceful and comforting place called marriage without sacrificing our grounding and reason.

To do this, I bring the stories, experience, and learning from many couples, colleagues, friends, and family. To all of those who have contributed their stories, their unwavering encouragement, and their wisdom, I thank you deeply.

To all the couples who have worked with me in counseling and have taught me so much, thank you. It has been a privilege to be taken into your confidence. I thank the couples who marry and make their best efforts to live meaningfully and lovingly; you are examples to us all.

Thank you to my family and friends who have read the manuscript at various stages and guided me with their insight and contributions. I thank my teachers and colleagues who have opened my eyes to new ways of looking at our complex human condition and helped me to be effective in my work.

This book could not have been possible without the help of Laura Golden Bellotti, who edited the original manuscript; Debora Carvalko, Senior Editor at Praeger Publishers, who believed in this project the first time she read it, and all those at Praeger Publishing who worked to bring this book to completion. I am sincerely grateful.

I wish to thank the contributors whose names appear in text, as well as those who have given me their permission to write about them anonymously. To protect their anonymity, the stories presented here have been disguised by changing the names, places, and situations. Other stories are either fictitious or conglomerations of several couples' experiences. Any similarity to an actual individual or couple is purely coincidental.

Finally, I would like to thank my mentors and friends, Dr. G. Andrew H. Benjamin and Dr. Avedis Panajian, who have been with me in my inner conversation throughout my personal development and the writing of this book.

Chapter 1

The Altered State of Being in Love

If you trust nothing else, trust this. Trust us.
—Arwen to Aragorn, *Lord of the Rings*

There are two forces that drive all human beings: the drive or instinct toward life, and the drive toward death. If we need evidence of our drive toward life, we need look no further than falling in love, being in love, and wanting to marry.

We enter a special state of mind when we fall in love, one in which all our creativity is activated. We are euphoric. Our senses are heightened. We are ready for anything. We feel inspired and up to any challenge, confident in who we are and what we can accomplish. Our nervous systems light up like Christmas trees, and we feel as high as if we'd drunk a potent dose of pheromones and endorphins. The machinery of our drive to life turns over in high gear, biological alarm clocks go off, and we suddenly feel the urge to make a baby, build a family, or put our best skills and creative energy to use to achieve our goals. Our lives seem richer and brimming with possibilities.

When we are in the throes of new love, we live fully in the present moment. We seem to cast off anchors from the past and worries concerning the future. Paradoxically, we want this present moment to last forever: We look forward to growing old together with our beloved. Aging no longer seems like something negative because now we have someone with whom to share a lifetime of anticipated achievements and rewards. And even if there are obstacles to overcome, we know we'll be able to face them courageously

"Air Castles," Maxfield Parrish. Photo courtesy Archives of the American Illustrators Gallery NYC, www. american illustrators.com © Copyright 2007 National Museum of American Illustration, Newport 02840, www.americanillustration.org.

with our loved one by our side. We have gained an inner strength and optimism that only love seems to deliver.

When we're in love with our potential mate, it feels as if our wish for lasting happiness has finally been fulfilled and that we have become the person we were meant to be. How did we fall into such a blissful state?

WHERE DOES LOVE BEGIN?

Our preparation for falling in love begins long before we meet our lover. We are conditioned by our families and our culture to believe in a lasting love that will define our lives. Literature, films, and popular songs instill fantasies of finding our one true love, enjoying the sweet pleasures and welcome comforts of a soul mate, and creating a home with the one we were meant to be with. When we're dating someone, we look for signs that he or she might be "the one," and if we think they might be, we strive to get closer to that person.

But years before we begin to date and fall in love, we learn what it means to need and receive love. Modern research is showing us just how early in our childhood our conception of love takes root. As infants and young children, we learn how to recognize love when we experience a parent's caring and comforting. Love is what makes us feel safe and nurtured. The subtle gestures of our earliest caregivers—usually our parents—signal us to feed and to cuddle, or, in the case of negative signals, to adapt to a dangerous or inhospitable environment. We carry these nonverbal memories, these intensely personal experiences with our caregivers, all the way into adulthood. When we seek a mate, we consciously or unconsciously look for someone with whom we can experience some of the same emotional interactions that we felt early in our lives. Sometimes we are even able to tell our partner what kinds of things they can do to make us feel loved.

There is a special moment when we first meet someone who might be a candidate for love when we may feel the pull of attraction. It is a moment of prerecognition and alertness, like an animal in the wild catching the first scent of a new creature, not yet knowing whether it is friend or foe. In the case of human beings, we wonder whether this feeling of being powerfully attracted to someone is love at first sight. Is "something in the way she moves me" enough in and of itself to call it love and to pursue marriage? For many of us it is: prerecognition or attraction, the inexplicable sense that "this is the one" leads directly to our decision to commit to this person. We say to ourselves, "She is beautiful, I want to be with her, I am in love," and we proceed directly from our senses and desires into action. For others, such attraction is just the first step, in which case we ask ourselves, "She is beautiful, and I want to be with her—could this develop into real love?"

When we fantasize about whether a relationship could be the real thing, we carry on an internal monologue, a running commentary that expands with each new experience with our potential partner. Our solitary fantasy of true love takes a quantum leap forward when we realize that our partner shares the same dream that this could be it. In this way, as a couple we create a shared fantasy, which then takes on more meaning and more power. In fact, partners often feel so empowered that they sense they are in an altered state.

Falling in love differs from other altered states of mind in two important ways. First, the state of just having fallen in love is more socially acceptable than being stoned or drunk. Family and friends generally recognize a newly-in-love couple's unusual behavior and make allowances for it. If the couple can't keep their hands off each other, feed each other at the table, or call each other pet names, those around them not only understand what's going on and accept the behavior, they may even think it's charming. Secondly, as each partner starts to identify himself as part of a couple, there is a birth of *us*—a new identity, complete with its own personality and the expectation that each partner will care for and nurture this new unit of two.

The new couple is intent on preserving their euphoria and protecting it from harm. Although the *us* identity is endearing, it is also self-involved, exclusive, hungry for acceptance, and hypersensitive to criticism. It needs to believe in itself and the rightness of its choices. As a personality type, the new *us* seems narcissistic in that it is self-absorbed and has a grandiose self-image. It is resistant to input from others and glorifies its point of view. The couple's *us* personality gleans tremendous satisfaction from experiencing its existence as essentially separate from the world. To some extent, these traits are completely appropriate to the age of the new couple, which is still in its infancy.

HOW DOES A NEWLY-IN-LOVE COUPLE ACT?

A couple in love is a powerful force of nature, capable of bringing about great change. Newly-in-love partners not only trust that they have the skills necessary to transform their dreams into reality, they optimistically believe that they can avoid the reality that love too often goes bad. Despite the divorce statistics that put the chances for a lasting marriage at 50 percent (or less if couples are remarrying, under stress such as military deployment, or blending families), only 10–16 percent of couples in the early stages of love believe that divorce could happen to *them*. This is largely because when we are newly in love, we feed our optimism with the euphoric good times we've experienced. And our culture, which glorifies romantic love, feeds that confidence as well. Since love is said to conquer all, partners who are "high on love" overlook conflicts in their relationship or flaws in their beloved and instead believe in the power of love to solve any problems that might arise. After all, John Lennon taught us that "All you need is love," and he may have been parroting Sophocles, who said, "One word frees us of all the weight and pain in life. That word is love."

Intuiting that *this could be it*, a newly-in-love couple reorganizes their world to give love its best chance. The new power of *us* disrupts their status quo and ripples through their established social network. Even the most rational and realistic among us become infused with hope and anxious happiness when we fall in love. We change whatever prior plans we might have made and realign our values to be in sync with the needs of the new *us*. In creating something wonderful, we sometimes neglect other aspects of our lives. We cancel dates with friends and neglect our chores. At work, we may think about how our work could better support our love rather than how we can do a better job. Our life appears to us in terms of black and white: there is our powerful and exhilarating new love, and then there is everything else.

"Everything else" is consigned to a holding area for the mundane, because our new love requires nearly all of our quality time. Given the choice, many of us would stay in this intoxicated phase indefinitely. But reality usually intrudes in the form of a neglected boss, landlord, or parent reminding us that commitments exist outside the realm of our all-consuming love. People in the early stages of love are responsive to others only when it is absolutely necessary. They are inwardly motivated, trusting in their own counsel and engaged in envisioning and building something greater than outsiders could ever imagine. There develops an "us versus them" mentality, as lovers seek only a positive reflection of their love and are defensive about any criticism of their state of mind or their newly beloved. On the other hand, when friends or relatives show even mild support of the new relationship, couples are strongly encouraged.

When partners are in the altered state of mind that falling in love brings about, they feel like radically different people—and their behavior reflects those feelings. They value things differently, make decisions differently, and their behavior changes in accordance with their new priorities. Acting in a grandiose fashion by making promises and extending favors to your loved one beyond what you would normally do makes perfect sense to a newly-in-love person. Yet the state of euphoria that promises lasting companionship and the opportunity to learn more and more about yourself and your mate has its drawbacks. Research indicates that we retain only 30 percent of what we learn in an altered state. Similarly, if we learn something when we're "straight," we will only recall 30 percent of it when we're high. How does this translate to the altered state of new love?

What we learn and how we feel about our lover when we are "high on love" is filtered through our optimistic, rose-colored glasses; but after marriage, when the glow of love is less intense, those feelings often shift. We build goodwill toward each other based on our loving, generous actions while we're both in a state of heightened arousal. When that arousal decreases, we may forget or discount that loving generosity, lower our expectations, and reassess our partner's behavior in terms of his or her current actions. We may think, "The two of us only acted that way initially because we were infatuated. Now I see the real person." We may not trust that the partner who seemed to love us so completely when we were infatuated with each other will continue to do so—and so we might withdraw protectively.

When this cooled-down period sets in, our loving, generous good-will needs to be reestablished in a more realistic context. Sometimes this means giving our partner the benefit of the doubt based on the good times we've already shared; or appreciating more subtle qualities we may have overlooked when we were in that initial altered state. In other words, we now spend time getting to know each other all over again from this new, relatively sober perspective. It's hard to really get to know someone when we're in the euphoria of new love, because we don't always act like ourselves. And we don't always give our lover an honest impression of who we are and what we value. Getting acquainted with a new love is tremendously exciting, but often being part of the new *us* means that we are so impatient to make our love permanent that we skip over the honest details of our lives. We project our expectations onto our partner and assume that they want what we want.

For most people in love, there is a defining moment when we recognize that this is the one for me. This is a sunshine moment. We tell ourselves, "This person is not only the object of my fantasy but also the perfect partner for me—someone with whom I can create the life I truly want." Now, plans can be made. Now, the wedding is really going to happen. If marriage counselors and psychologists were called upon to give advice at this point, they would suggest that there are a number of developmental milestones to be reached before announcing an engagement. These are detailed in the following chapters and involve finding out how compatible you are in general ways, such as personality types, and more specific ways, such as managing day-to-day married life; planning for your financial partnership; and clarifying your individual and jointly held goals, your relationships with extended family and in-laws, and your decision-making and communication styles.

In general, such advice is wholly ignored, and the couple often feels an increased anxiety as the result of even bringing up such unromantic, practical subjects. It's like finding a stone in your garden and having someone tell you to turn it over because there is something important underneath it. But you don't, because you're afraid that what you'll find will be threatening.

So the engagement goes forward.

In publicly declaring your love for each other and announcing your intention to commit yourselves to one another forever, you give your feelings the grand status that the two of you have already privately envisioned. Dramatic announcements of an engagement may surprise friends and family, but if others are skeptical, you may dismiss them with the hope that "they will see in time" how right the two of you are for each other. The sheer will and charisma of you two as a couple can sway dissenters and carry marriage plans forward. You may already consider yourselves married in the deepest sense, since your psychological marriage precedes your legal one.

As for premarital counseling or friendly advice from others, engaged couples usually want to hear only about their strengths, not about issues or struggles that may threaten them or undermine their dreams.

THE URGE TO LEGITIMIZE: MARRIAGE LICENSE AS TRANSITIONAL OBJECT

As you face the stress of blending your lives and adjusting to your new identity as *us*, you need reassurance that everything is going to work out the way you both envision it. Couples generally adapt to this need by establishing codes for emotional and physical behavior. Many of us also feel the need for concrete evidence of our commitment to the relationship. This new world of *us* is a jointly created fantasy that relies on receiving tangible proof from each other—in the form of engagement rings and a marriage license—that we indeed belong together. These highly regarded tokens of commitment are meant to encourage each partner to follow through with their plans.

But a marriage contract involves more than just the two of you. When a couple agrees to sign one, it means that their jointly created fantasy is now placed under the jurisdiction of state authorities. There is now a third party, the state, which also has a say in what their relationship will be like. The marriage contract is an intrusion on the fantasy created by the couple; yet, it is a welcomed one because it legitimizes the relationship in the eyes of the couple and the outside world.

Wanting to marry does not mean that a couple is ready for, or has even considered, the legal or moral implications of marriage. Nor does a couple's intention to marry necessarily mean that their ideas about marriage are the same, although when we are in love we are inclined to believe that they are. So what does the act of getting married really mean? It signifies the wish to be recognized as legitimately united, and it serves to comfort and reassure each partner that they are not alone.

A couple's desire to be legitimized has to do with their emotional bond; the marriage contract gives that bond socially acceptable phrasing so that the couple can continue living within their fantasy of lasting love and security. Like a security blanket, the marriage contract seems to protect their romance from dissipating, but it doesn't necessarily mean that the couple has considered the realities of marriage.

I often refer to a marriage license as a transitional object. It was pediatrician and psychoanalyst Donald Winnicott who first wrote about the significance of transitional objects. When a young child is learning to separate from his mother, such objects as a treasured blanket or stuffed animal can provide comfort and security until the baby has developed an internal image of his mother. Before he can hold his mother in his mind, the child needs his "blankey" as a substitute for his mother's love and protection. Otherwise, when the mother is gone, the baby feels abandoned. This fear of abandonment is intolerable to the young child, so the special blanket becomes an irreplaceable prop, a surrogate for Mom.

A marriage license is a very special piece of paper signifying a couple's certainty that they are in love, as well as the social expectation that they will love, honor, and cherish one another forever. Along with a wedding ring, it serves as a transitional object by symbolizing that you are part of a cherished couple, the *us* you so carefully created during courtship. Being married, signified by the contract and ring, warms and reassures you even in your partner's absence. And it indicates to others that you are not single; you have a special status as a married person and should be treated accordingly.

You are more than yourself alone; you are also a husband or a wife, and you live under the auspices of society, as well as your personal religious beliefs. You belong to all of these things, even when your partner is not standing physically by your side.

Just as a blankey is only a symbol of maternal love, a marriage license is only a symbol of a couple's intention to love and cherish each other forever. It can't actually ensure or preserve your love. Unfortunately, too often couples are unaware of the ways in which their envisioned life together can clash with the legal and religious definitions of marriage. Which is why it is so important for you to consider the "fine print" of the marriage contract prior to saying "I do." If you want your marriage to be held together by more than a transitional object, it is wise to confront the full spectrum of issues that you'll be faced with as husband and wife. One way to do this is to read this book; another is to engage in couples counseling as early as 6 months before the ceremony (perhaps after the engagement, but definitely before the wedding invitations go out!) so that both of you can explore those aspects of marriage that are critical to a healthy and happy relationship.

Until both of you feel confident that you have adequately explored the realities of being married, as well as the strengths and weaknesses you each bring to the relationship, you risk feeling as insecure about your marriage as a baby feels without his "blankey." And you'll likely feel ultrasensitive about receiving premarital feedback from friends and family.

UNWANTED ADVICE VERSUS EMOTIONAL SUPPORT

Family and friends often give unwanted advice to newly-in-love couples in an attempt to get them to see their relationship in more objective or realistic terms. Since these mostly well-meaning loved ones may fear that your idealistic notion of love will ultimately hurt you, they hope to spare you the punishment Goethe referred to when he said, "Love is an ideal thing. Marriage is a real thing. A confusion of the real with the ideal never goes unpunished." Other family members and friends may refrain from commenting on the bond between you and your partner for fear they might risk losing their own relationship with one or the other of you.

There are additional risks in giving unwelcome advice. Research indicates that the perceived disapproval of parents creates a problem in the marriage, because social acceptance is so important to us. However, parental disapproval doesn't affect a couple's marital satisfaction, which is what determines the success of a marriage. Having an added problem and not having it affect the happiness of your marriage may seem contradictory, but it's not. That's because the ability to work out problems between the two of you is what's most important. When others point out a problem, it doesn't mean that you'll be less satisfied in your marriage, but it does add to your burden because (1) the two of you may not accept that the particular issue is a problem; (2) it represents the disapproval of a loved one; and (3) it doesn't contribute to your ability as a couple to recognize, manage, and resolve problems when they come up. It is the latter capability that determines marital satisfaction.

All couples have problems, and it doesn't necessarily help to hear someone point them out. It can help, however, when someone (preferably outside of the family) points out a problem as an example of how the two of you can work together to overcome it. If a problem is truly insurmountable, a third party such as a premarital or marriage counselor can guide you to maintain integrity and manage your differences so that the problem doesn't overwhelm the love and good-will you feel for each other.

Is there any welcome advice that well-meaning friends or relatives might give to a newly-in-love or engaged couple? We surveyed 100 young adults to find out how they felt when friends and relatives gave them feedback about their relationships. Here are some of the things they said they appreciated hearing or would have liked to hear:

- "Hold on to this one!"
- "You make a nice couple."
- "We support you as long as you're happy."
- "He's your kind of guy, but if he breaks your heart I'll break his neck."
- I liked hearing that my parents trust me to make the right choice in a partner.
- I appreciated hearing that they think we're good for each other.
- I would like to hear that my friends are a little bit jealous.
- I liked hearing that they thought they could be friends with him.
- I liked that my parents were impressed by how polite my fiancé is with them.
- I appreciated that they know how much she means to me.

Those who made the above comments seemed to want corroboration that their judgment is sound and that their choices are adult and success-oriented.

Here are some things that couples said they *don't* want to hear from friends and family:

- "He's a troublemaker, a bad influence."
- "We don't trust him."
- "He's all wrong for you!"
- "You don't look right together."
- "She cheated on you."
- "He's taking you away from your other friendships."
- "He/she's a loser."
- "You deserve better."

- "You don't know what love is."
- "You're taking it too fast."
- "You probably won't last long."
- "You're being conned."
- "She's only with you because she feels sorry for you."
- "Are you pregnant?" (Implying that's the only reason we're planning to get married.)
- Anything mean or derogatory about the person I've chosen to love.
- Giving me the "third degree" about him.

Quite obviously, the above comments indicate that friends and family feel the couple's judgment is not sound and that they can't be trusted to make wise decisions.

When couples were asked how they would prefer to have others approach them about their relationship, here's what they said:

- I wouldn't want people to say anything bad about my relationship or put me on the spot.
- I would prefer that people be direct, not beat around the bush.
- I would only want a friend to say something negative if there was a secret that I really needed to know, like my boyfriend was cheating.
- I would want friends or family to tell me how they felt, but I wouldn't want them to hurt my feelings.
- I would want my friend to tell me if she thought I might be opening myself up to getting hurt.
- I wouldn't want friends or family to say anything, because it would make me feel that I'm irresponsible and make bad choices.

Overall, the above comments reveal that newly-in-love couples can be very sensitive when it comes to friends and family voicing their opinions about their relationship. The feedback couples get from those who know them best reflects a general sense of trust or distrust, well-wishes or ill-wishes, support or lack of support. Pre-wed couples are primarily interested in how friends and family can support them. You want to feel worthy of your parents' and friends' trust, and you want your judgment in choosing a mate to be validated. You want approval, but not too much of it (which could also be threatening.) And if you are in relationships with parents, siblings, or friends where intimate details of your lives are not shared or harsh criticism is anticipated, then you are likely predisposed to discount the opinions of others, and exaggerate your own.

All of these are reasons why it is so important for you to fully explore and understand your own feelings about why you're getting married and what you expect from your partner, your relationship, and yourself. If you find yourself feeling defensive about other people's advice and feedback prior to your wedding—or if you need others to validate your own feelings about your fiancé, that's a sign that you may be insecure about your relationship. Is there a small or large threat to your relationship that you're not acknowledging? The *us* that you've created with your partner may so want this new love to succeed that it is thwarting an honest examination of your bond. It doesn't feel good to be criticized, but is it possible to consider the criticism objectively? When you ask yourself the following question, how do you honestly respond?

"Is there something about this relationship that I should look at and judge for myself, in case it poses a real threat to our love?"

HOW DO YOUR PAST EXPERIENCES OF LOVE AFFECT YOUR PRE-WED RELATIONSHIP?

Once a lover becomes our spouse-to-be, the attachment we feel for that person begins to share certain important qualities with other past intimate relationships in which we were dependent, interdependent, cared for, or caring. In forming this new attachment, we open a channel, which transfers some of the dynamics of our previous relationships into this one. Like bridges across the same body of water, the emotional traffic of our current relationship and those we've had in the past runs in both directions, and it's sometimes hard to keep the messages straight. Marriage can complicate our lives by allowing an association between our new spouse and those people from our past who have occupied a similar role in our lives.

It happens like this: A particular situation triggers you or your partner to respond to the other *as if* they were someone from your past, someone with enough emotional resonance to commandeer the present and interrupt your honest, present-tense exchange. This "someone from your past" could be your primary caregiver (usually your mother or father, with whom you formed a primary attachment in infancy) or a previous partner, even a sibling. Someone with whom you have had an important relationship and an established manner of relating. In our newly-in-love state of mind, we are quick to recognize in our new lover the positive traits we either yearned for or valued in others from our past. In so doing, we may exaggerate the positive qualities of our newly beloved and neglect the differences between us.

When we relate to our present partner with the emotional remnants of past relationships, it's as if we're living with ghosts. Instead of connecting with our spouse-to-be, we project onto them qualities we missed growing up, or we misunderstand each other due to our previous assumptions about what love is and how it works.

For instance, Julia grew up assuming that taking care of someone was the way to receive love. The oldest of four children, she was expected to look after her siblings like a surrogate mother, and in return she received approval—and what she felt as love—from her parents. She thus grew up unconsciously expecting that by taking care of someone, she would receive love in return. While it is common during courtship for a partner to overextend him or herself to try to please the other person, Julia's caretaking of Rick left a false impression. When they were newly in love, Rick appreciated the elaborate meals Julia made for him, and he took pleasure in how she showered him with attention, demonstrating her constant concern for his well-being. He assumed that this was simply Julia's way of showing her love for him and that she enjoyed treating him in this way. What he was unaware of, however, was that Julia also expected him to eventually return the favors. In her experience, love involved caretaking, and she hoped Rick would one day do for her not only what she'd done for him but what she'd done for her sisters as well. For his part, Rick was unaware of the emotional debt he'd been running up; in their blissful, altered state of love he and Julia never talked about what they expected from one another or what love actually meant to either of them.

In Bret and Gail's case, the effects from a past relationship were triggered by a certain look in Gail's eyes. We often misinterpret subtle, nonverbal cues from each other, especially when we don't know someone that well. And that's what happened with Bret. One of the things he was attracted to in Gail was the unflinching attention she paid him whenever they were having a conversation. She would maintain constant eye contact with him, projecting an open, loving regard. Bret felt that Gail was completely attentive and available to him, a sure sign of her love. In fact, Gail's attentive gaze had a very different meaning. Her previous relationship had been with an abusive man, who slapped her across the face when they argued, often demanding that Gail "Look at me when I'm talking to you!" She had thus been conditioned to face the object of her anxiety without conveying any fear or withdrawal. What Gail was really communicating to Bret was that she was beyond being hurt. Her focused look actually projected a sense of defiance, not love. When they came in for couples counseling, Bret and Gail discovered how incorrect their initial assessments of each other had been. Bret saw her gaze as signaling unguarded availability; Gail saw him as a man who couldn't threaten her.

It is a constant struggle to remain present, to be attentive to the intentions and actions of one's partner, to question what they mean rather than assume that they are acting as so-and-so did in the past. When our established patterns of relating are healthy and positive, we hope our partner will behave similarly; but if he or she doesn't, we are open to disagreement and disappointment. For instance, we need to tell ourselves, "Okay, so my fiancé doesn't understand that what I really want from him right now is a shoulder to cry on. Given my upbringing and my past relationships, this is the behavior I anticipated. But I obviously have to talk to him about this."

If we take the time to examine our own expectations, we have a chance to see if they are fair, realistic, and in our best interest. Perhaps our partner is offering a new way to manage a particular situation—that's just as good as or better than the way we interacted with people in our past. Or maybe we unfairly expect something of our partner because we lacked it in our family of origin. If we're open enough to talk to our mate about our expectations and flexible enough to alter them, we can become more clear about what we value, what pleases us, and what is in both of our best interests to expect.

Some people claim that they enter a relationship without expectations. I believe that is impossible. We may be unconscious of our expectations, but we all have them. By becoming more aware of what we expect from our relationship, we have an opportunity to learn about ourselves and to grow as individuals and as a couple.

LOVE'S IMPOSTER AND THE COURAGE TO LOOK YOUR RELATIONSHIP IN THE FACE

Despite the fact that love is a creative force, it is hard for most of us to describe it—which is why we're so grateful when poets do so for us. We feel the need to express our feelings of love, but whether or not we can put those feelings into words, we know we're in love when we're in it, or at least we think we do.

Unfortunately, because love seems to be so intuitive and irrational, we risk being vulnerable to something that feels like love, but isn't. I call this other state of being *love's imposter*. Love's imposter is something divorced couples can describe in great detail; but if you're aware of the imposter before you get married, you'll be less likely to follow in the divorcee's footsteps.

If we return to Freud's first principle, that love is a creative drive, we can look at the effects of what we're calling love to see if they are creative or destructive. If the effects of "this thing called love" are creative—if we find ourselves more energized and successful in our day-to-day lives; if our efforts lead to greater satisfaction for ourselves, our families, and our work; if our goals and dreams become more attainable, because the two of us labor together in our own way—then we can feel secure that we are indeed experiencing real love. If, on the other hand, the effects of our relationship are destructive, then we should ask ourselves, "What is this thing that looks like love, feels like love, but because of the negative consequences it has produced, cannot possibly be love?" The answer: It must be love's imposter.

When we talk about love's imposter, we're referring to that aspect of ourselves that defends against the growth that inevitably comes with trying new things, expanding ourselves, and testing our courage. The imposter is the expression of the death instinct, what many psychologists believe is our resistance to the dangerous, unpredictable learning experiences that life throws our way. It is that force within us that counsels us to retreat, to stop learning, to ruminate on the past. The death instinct persuades us not to risk the pain of trying and possibly failing at a new endeavor, especially one so complex as love. Love's imposter, which reflects this no-growth instinct, seduces but does not satisfy; consumes but does not renew.

To rush headlong and recklessly into a marriage without knowing fully what love and marriage mean is often a sign that you're in the grip of love's imposter. But it's natural to resist testing the authenticity of "this thing called love," because we feel we have so much to lose. Love—or its clever imposter—seems to give us so much pleasure, why would we want to jeopardize that? If love conquers all, why rock the boat by asking our partner how he or she feels about family budgets, adoption, stay-at-home dads and moms, religious practices, or that great taboo: a prenuptial agreement? Why confront his or her troubling behavior, which you're hoping will go away once marital bliss takes over? It may seem preferable to protect your love from potential harm, savoring every precious moment, than to risk uncovering some hidden blemish that could undo it all.

Once we become engaged, we feel we're so close to having all that love promises. Why invite a snake into the garden?

But is learning more about how our partner feels and what marriage holds in store for us really so evil? We don't avoid consulting with a business advisor prior to initiating a new start-up company. And we wouldn't neglect to double-check our proposal before giving it to a client. In the business world, it is standard operating procedure to substantiate our choices and actions. So why do we object to rationally assessing our relationship before getting married? Why do so many of us avoid seeking outside consultation for the most important decision of our lives?

It is the jointly created *us* that often avoids troubling questions about our partner or our relationship. The resistance to exploring with your partner what marriage means to each of you suggests that there is a fear that your love is too fragile, unable to withstand any potential differences or clashes. But it is an act of courage to engage in good-faith planning prior to your wedding, to not only face up to problems and concerns but to discuss your ideas concerning finances, morality, career, and children.

I will respectfully raise these issues with you throughout the course of this book. We will explore underlying conflicts between you and your partner, as well as the special skills and coping strategies that can help you work out your differences over the long term. Think of this book as a premarital journey—one that will prepare you for the lifelong adventure you're about to embark on.

Chapter 2

A Good-enough Match?

Realizing that our relationship isn't perfect but "good enough" is not the same thing as "settling." To me, settling means there's a part of you that's impatient, a part that sadly believes this is all you deserve, a part that thinks that the lover of your dreams is either pure fantasy or already taken by someone else. I know some people settle because they're desperate to be with someone, or to leave home, or to have a baby. But when Brad and I decided to get married, it wasn't about settling. We had a long enough engagement so that we both realized we could be really happy with each other, that together we could learn and grow and comfort each other through good times and bad. That was good enough for me!

—Jennifer, married 6 years

What do you expect from your partner and from marriage? If you're like many young couples, you may feel that you and your spouse-to-be are a perfect match and that your future life together is destined to play out perfectly. In your current state of premarital bliss, you may believe that there's no need to talk over boring specifics about sharing a bank account, changing careers, or bringing up kids with your religion rather than your partner's. After all, you expect that love will conquer all.... Or maybe you and your partner don't define your emotional state as necessarily blissful; still, you love each other and are looking forward to getting married. In your case, the two of you haven't discussed your marital expectations because, well..., you really have no expectations. You're getting married, you trust your partner, and you figure that whatever problems arise will somehow be reasonably resolved.

Although you may think that the word "expectations" has a negative ring, knowing what you expect and want from marriage is a good thing. When we're clear about our expectations, we're much more apt to achieve our goals and be satisfied with the life we've built. On the other hand, if we are unclear about what we want, nothing will ever seem good enough. Our desires will be aimless, and we'll wind up constantly hungering for more than we have.

In this chapter, we'll begin by focusing on your expectations—of your partner and of marriage. We're going to get clear about not only realistic versus blissful expectations but also what's actually in the back of your mind when you say you have no expectations at all.

Since the one expectation most pre-weds have is that their marriage will last—even though divorce statistics are disheartening—we're also going to confront those stats and talk about "good-enough" marriages. Just as overanxious moms and dads are advised to stop trying to be perfect parents and to instead become "good-enough" ones, I'll advise you to think about your relationship in terms of being good-enough. By that I don't mean settling for someone you don't love; I mean having what it takes to create a happy, lifelong marriage. In the course of this chapter, you'll get the chance to assess your relationship and discover if it is a "good-enough match." To help you figure that out, we'll consider what current research reveals about who is most likely to have a satisfying and long-lasting marriage.

But first...

WHAT DO YOU EXPECT?

Most of us expect our partner to love, honor, and cherish us, or we would not ask them to take the marriage vows. But can't loving, honoring, and cherishing be demonstrated in a range of different behaviors? For example, being physically affectionate; showing compassion; being a good listener; taking care of you when you're sick; respecting your ideas or plans even when they differ from your partner's. Which of those behaviors do you expect from your future spouse?

On the other hand, aren't there some behaviors that you absolutely expect your partner *never* to engage in—like spousal abuse?

Beyond demonstrating that they love us, and not harming us physically, what else do we expect of our mates? The following are some common expectations that come under the umbrella of compatibility. As you consider these, see if you can begin to zero-in on your own specific marital desires and standards.

- I expect sexual compatibility and "chemistry" between us.
- I expect us to get along on a daily basis.

- I expect us to be able to manage an argument without "going nuclear"—and to make up when it's over.
- I expect us to be in agreement on the important stuff—like having (or not having) kids and planning for our future.
- I expect us to agree on how to manage our money.
- I expect my partner to care about my family.
- I expect us to trust each other and to be there for each other.
- I expect my partner to respect me.
- I expect my partner to be faithful.

Overall, we expect our mate to be compatible in many ways—physically, emotionally, socially, and practically. Whether we're aware of it or not, we enter into marriage with a long list of unspoken expectations. When we don't acknowledge our expectations or share them with our mate, misunderstandings and conflicts can arise.

In the following story, Rick, married for 15 years to Annie, talks about how he envisioned their marriage and how that initial vision contrasted with the realities of their relationship. While some of his expectations were accurate—he and Annie were very compatible in many ways—he concedes that he never expected to have to be so careful around Annie when they disagree. Their experience points to the benefits of revealing your expectations to your future mate, even when you believe you're a near-perfect match.

When I met Annie it was love at first sight, but I've spent years adjusting to our different ways. Don't get me wrong, I am truly lucky in love. It helped that we came from similar backgrounds and our parents knew each other and approved of our marriage. I guess I felt that they'd done some of the "prescreening" for me. I was grateful, because all I wanted to do was to be in love with Annie for as many years as we could manage.

One day, in our brief courtship, we went for a four-hour walk and talked about everything we had in mind for ourselves and our marriage. I was amazed; we were in complete agreement about everything. Annie doesn't remember that conversation at all now and chides me for making the whole thing up. Still, in our many years together we have done everything as we discussed that day. I guess she doesn't need to remember the day to believe in the things we said, that's how honest we were with each other.

I'd like to think that if we'd disagreed, we could have talked about it. But we didn't have that opportunity, being of such like-minds. Also, neither of us really knew how to talk about disagreements respectfully, because we'd never seen a discussion like that in either of our families. When I lived at home with my parents, it was more like my father crowing about being the master of the house, until my mother quietly went into the kitchen and started breaking dishes. Then she would get her way. If that's what honest discussions were like, then I had had enough of them.

Although my wife and I agree on most issues, we go about doing things much differently. I'm the diplomat of the family and try to smooth things over. Annie has a different approach. She can be like a she-lion when it comes to protecting her family or defending herself against slights from disrespectful service people, or bad drivers, or people who criticize our children. I try to reason with our kids as best I can, but Annie is more apt to command them, which is sometimes hard for them to accept. And even when they do it her way (which is most often a good way, if not the best) there is some distance created between the kids and her. They value her advice, but are afraid of the strong words and tone of voice she uses to get the message across.

I love them all, my wife and my children. I guess my role has always been to try to get them to see each other's point of view.

For Annie and I, it's not so much our differences of opinion that's the problem, but the way we come across to each other. I have so wanted peace in my marriage that I shied away from ever confronting her. I guess I feared that when I started standing up for myself, she would go into the kitchen and start breaking dishes. That sound of dishes breaking in anger still haunts me, still scares me as if I were still a little boy in my mother's kitchen. My heart would pump loudly in my chest imagining Annie's response if I were to disagree with her.

But things have changed for me. I'm older now, and I don't have the patience to always be a diplomat. I find that I can get angry too—like when I can't complete a sentence without Annie interrupting me—and I'm less apt to "let things slide" for the sake of keeping the peace.

But I've been surprised by Annie's reaction to the "new" me. She still went toe-to-toe with me about things that mattered to her, but she began to treat me differently, more respectfully. She started to defer to me in front of the kids, whereas before, she always took control. I guess she thought my diplomacy was weakness. I now realize that she has needed me to take a stand on things so that she wouldn't have to be in control of everything on her own. If, before we got married, we could have talked about what would happen if we were to disagree, maybe my expectations wouldn't have been so unrealistic. How could I have ever thought that things would always go as smoothly as they had in those first months of being madly in love?

I feel much less afraid to speak my mind now. I don't have that constant need to be tactful. Interestingly, I can tell that Annie is happier with me now. She takes my arm more readily when we go out, and she's taken to calling me pet names again, which has been a welcome surprise.

Because Rick and Annie never disagreed about anything when they were pre-weds, they never had the opportunity to discover core aspects of their individual personalities. They assumed that they each meant the same thing when they vowed to love, honor, and cherish each other; however, their story highlights the importance of considering what our marriage vows actually mean to each of us. What does it mean for your partner to promise to love you? In what ways do you expect him (or her) to demonstrate that he cherishes you? When he vows to honor you, how do you expect him to show it? By standing up for you when you need support? By honoring a common goal even if it means accepting the fact that you go about it in a way that is perhaps distasteful to him? When you think about the marital model your parents provided you with, can you identify a problem they had and discuss it with your partner—to see if there's a chance it might repeat itself in your upcoming marriage?

In the following story, Pam talks of having "talked about everything" before she and Reggie married. But she also admits to an unacknowledged expectation: that Reggie, a quiet man who doesn't talk very much, would come to her and talk over any problems he was having with their relationship. That didn't happen. Here's what did:

Before we got married, we talked about everything. I couldn't believe there was any part of our future that we hadn't planned out. It was all going to be perfect, from the wedding cake to the honeymoon to the planned family, career and two-week vacation every year. I could hardly believe my luck—everyone in our families approved of our marriage and welcomed us into each other's homes. I never expected that our life would turn out so differently...

Reggie and I both worked for a federal agency that set our work schedule in an unusual way. He was a forest ranger who would go out in the field for ten days on, four days off all season. I worked forestry too, but got to come home every night. For the first few years, everything worked out better than I could've hoped. We enjoyed our time away from each other (although sometimes I would run up the backcountry trails to surprise him with an overnight visit) and we really cherished our time together. It seemed like our honeymoon was extended because of our frequent separations, and I couldn't wait for him to come home. He was a quiet man (while I tend to talk a lot) but I always assumed that he would talk to me if there was a problem. There was certainly no problem discussing the little day-to-day glitches and finding ways to help each other. I was totally blindsided when I found out the truth.

For years, people had been telling me "absence makes the heart grow fonder" until I met an old fisherman who finished the adage for me, "Absence makes the heart grow fonder—for somebody else!" Ridiculous, I thought. Until it seemed like everyone in town knew about Reggie's affair but me.

When I confronted him, he seemed to skate around the issue. When I finally pinned him down, he admitted to having an affair and more;

that he wanted to be with her full-time. He didn't ask for a divorce because we were settled nicely in our house and he didn't want to rock the boat. I was flabbergasted! How poorly he knew me, how little he thought of me, that I could be the other woman, keep his home, and spend my nights wondering if he was with her! What did he expect of me, to be his doormat?

Our marriage ended 15 years ago now. My son (it's still hard to call him "our" son, since his father was never around) is my pride and joy and has made the sacrifices completely worthwhile. It just seems ironic that someone like me, who planned everything in advance, could have been so unprepared for this: single and middle aged, with so little of the comfort and camaraderie that I originally hoped for.

Reggie and Pam had different expectations that appear obvious in retrospect: Pam expected that they would talk over any problems that would arise and that Reggie would be faithful. And he expected that his time away from Pam was his business—and that infidelity was somehow okay. So, how did they miss such glaring red flags? Were they so infatuated initially that they believed love would conquer all? Or were the issues never brought up, in conversation or in counseling, so that each partner was left to believe that there were no issues? Did Reggie and Pam assume that they had so much in common they didn't need to discuss the details of managing a marriage?

Perhaps, in premarital counseling sessions, these issues could have been raised for them. Careful questioning might have revealed differences in their attitudes and expectations. The assumption in premarital couples counseling is that, prior to marriage, both partners are open to being honest about such things, given their love-altered state of mind. In counseling, psychological tools and questionnaires are carefully developed to expose differences that warrant discussion. Sometimes, they expose a person's beliefs that are a surprise even to himself.

Since couples cannot avoid the issues that are bound to come up in the course of a lifetime together, in premarital counseling they have the opportunity to face issues that might not arise naturally for years. Counseling is like compressing time to see a likely, realistic outcome of a marriage. Sometimes, the process can seem like a pressure-cooker; when seemingly insurmountable issues arise, couples may wish to bolt from therapy, preferring to turn away from that disturbing reflection rather than use it to mold a relationship that could work. But more often, couples come away with important insights about themselves, their partner, and how they interact—which can help them navigate the road ahead.

We all want marriage to work. So let's consider what we expect from a wife or husband to see how compatible we really are.

YOUR MARITAL EXPECTATIONS—AN INTERACTIVE EXERCISE

Now that you're more aware of what can happen when pre-weds don't share their marital expectations, perhaps you'll be inspired to be more open with your spouse-to-be. Here are some guidelines for this exercise:

1) Set ground rules for your disclosure to each other. Do each of you expect complete disclosure—or are there certain things you don't want to discuss with each other? Decide between the two of you what needs to be disclosed and what doesn't, so that you both feel comfortable doing this exercise.

2) First write down your expectations concerning the general role of a husband or wife. Then write down your specific expectations in each of the following categories: the role of husband and wife, physical, emotional, practical, social, and parenting. In order for this exercise to be really useful, your "I expect" statements should be specific and personal. I have offered a few examples in each category to give you some jumping-off points.

3) Share your lists with your partner. The interesting part of this exercise will be the responses that you and your partner give to each other concerning the other person's expectations—and the negotiation that ensues. For example, if one partner states "I expect us to have sex at least three times a week," the possible responses and negotiations might be one of these:

   a. That's what I expect too!

   b. That feels like a lot of pressure on me to perform. If I'm not up for it, will you feel disappointed or betrayed?

   c. Can we leave room to negotiate, since sex is so important to us both? For instance, can we agree on the things that can make us more open to making love—like candles, music, babysitters, and forgetting about chores?

   d. I would like to make love to you three times a week. If we can't, then I need to connect with you intimately to find out why we're not. If I can make a connection with you by talking, then that might be enough for me. I just can't stand being rejected, not knowing why, and not knowing how to get closer to you.

   e. There's no way I can promise to have sex three times a week. Having an obligation or schedule for sex is not how I want our sex life to be.

If one of you responds "no way" to the other's expectations, that's where the exercise gets interesting, because that's when the negotiation begins! You will then need to ask yourselves such questions as: How important is that particular expectation to me and to my spouse? Is the expectation reasonable or unreasonable? Can we work out a compromise? For matters other than sex, is it possible for us to have some of our needs and expectations met outside of the relationship without violating our agreements? For example, would a "girl's night out" satisfy my need for camaraderie? Would a professional therapeutic massage satisfy his need to relieve stress, and free up our sex life to be more mutually pleasing and loving?

Here are samples of "I Expect" lists.

A Husband's and Wife's Role

I expect a husband to financially support his wife.

I expect a wife to earn an income.

I expect a husband to be a best friend.

I expect a wife to respect what I do for a living.

Physical Expectations

I expect us to have sex at least three times a week.

I expect us to continue to be experimental in our lovemaking.

I expect you to kiss me or give me a hug when you come home from work.

Emotional Expectations

I expect you to be empathetic when I've had a hard day.

I expect you not to be mean or harsh with me, even when you're angry.

I expect you to accept my occasional moodiness.

Practical Expectations

I expect us to have a savings plan and to stay out of debt.

I expect us to share household chores.

I expect us to make financial decisions jointly.

Social Expectations

I expect us to take at least one vacation a year together.

I expect to be able to take separate vacations with my friends occasionally.

I expect us to get together with friends and have fun on the weekend.

I expect us to celebrate some holidays together as a couple and some with our families.

Parenting Expectations

I expect us to wait at least 3 years before having children.

I expect us to each take an equal role in raising our children.

I expect us to raise our children within a religious tradition.

I expect you to be a caring stepparent to my children from a previous marriage.

WEDDING NIGHT EXPECTATIONS

Although your wedding night is only the first in a lifetime of nights together, pre-weds often have highly charged expectations of how that night should go. What do you expect, or at least hope for, on your wedding night? Do you expect to have mad, passionate sex? Do you expect the experience to be especially long lasting and romantic? Some partners take for granted that memorable sex will be part of their wedding night, others look on it as a duty. But if you listen to stories of newlyweds, sex on the wedding night doesn't always come off as planned. Between the high expectations, the overwhelming stimulation from a big celebration, the endless champagne toasts, and the odd encounters with distant relatives, by the time you leave the party, one of you may not be in the mood for sex. If that's the case, sex may lack the passion you were expecting.

You might want to consider ways to take the pressure off such high expectations by telling each other something like this: "When the party is over, I really want to make love to you, but I'm afraid I might be done in by all the preparation and celebrating. I'd hate to let you down if you're really counting on it. If we're too tired that night, would it be okay if we went to bed and made love in the morning?"

WHAT IS A GOOD-ENOUGH MATCH?

In the classic story *Fiddler on the Roof*, Tevya's daughters plead with the matchmaker to either find them a perfect match or leave them alone. Fearing a lifelong commitment to a spouse who might not meet their expectations, the young women proclaim that unless they can pair up with a "matchless match," they prefer to remain single. They sing,

> Matchmaker, Matchmaker, you know that I'm
> Still very young. Please, take your time.
> Up to this minute, I misunderstood
> That I could get stuck for good ...
>
> Matchmaker, matchmaker, plan me no plans ...
> Find me no find, catch me no catch.
> Unless he's a matchless match!
> (lyrics by Sheldon Harnick)

If we expect our marriage to last until death do us part, don't we want to make sure that we've made at least a near-perfect match? But what does that really mean? What qualities are necessary for a relationship to go the distance and beat the odds against divorce? Since no match is perfect, the psychological literature rarely discusses marital *bliss*, focusing instead on marital *satisfaction*. Bliss seems to be confined to the honeymoon-phase of marriage, a time when we are essentially free from conflict, and when our individual differences are overlooked due to our urge to merge.

But conflict isn't necessarily a barrier to a happy marriage. John Gottman talks about how conflict is a normal and healthy part of marriage. In fact, he found that successful marriages had the same level of conflict as unsuccessful ones. The difference was in how the conflicts were managed. We'll learn more about that in the next section on marital harmony.

Other than knowing how to manage conflicts, what else do couples need to insure that their marriages have a shot at lasting a lifetime? Research indicates that couples with *traditional* values are most successful at having lifelong marriages. However, closer examination of traditional couples, who represent 23 percent of those surveyed, reveals that although their marriages lasted longer, their group had the highest percentage of less-happy marriages (50%) (Fowers, Montel, & Olson 1996).

So if we want our marriages to be both happy and long-lasting, what does it take? Just as parents learn that they don't have to be perfect parents in order to raise healthy children, couples don't have to have a perfect marriage in order to have a happy, healthy one. They just need a good-enough one. In the next four sections, each of which profiles a particular theory about success in marriage, we'll weigh the importance of these and other factors:

- A couple's level of expressed emotion
- How couples resolve conflicts
- Partners' ability to trust, based on their early bonding with parents
- Similar outlook on the world
- Similar way of relating to others
- Similarity of healthy family backgrounds
- Closeness to one's father
- Compatible personalities, attitudes, beliefs, and values
- Consensus building and shared "relationship ground rules"

Wow...quite a long list, right? Perhaps this is why we need a long-enough engagement to have time to discuss and discover all the things that go into a satisfying marriage. The number of things to consider can be daunting. Again, these factors were found to be important by four different theories and four different teams of researchers. So let's take a look at each theory, and see how they might apply to you and your soon-to-be mate.

BALANCING PERCEPTION, EMOTIONAL RESPONSE, AND COMMUNICATION

According to John Gottman, harmony in a marriage is achieved when there is a balance in three core areas of a relationship: *perception, emotional response*, and *communication*. Each core area interacts with and overlaps the others. So changes in one area can cause repercussions in another. Also, each area has a negative threshold that, when exceeded, destabilizes the marriage.

For example, a husband is doing the dishes and places a cast iron skillet on the kitchen counter. His wife says, "Why don't you put a towel under that so it doesn't scratch the counter?" Her perception is that she's being helpful. He, on the other hand, still carries a grudge against her for micromanaging his life in other ways, so his perception of what just happened is quite different, and he responds to her in a snippy tone of voice, "Can't you let me do anything without trying to control me?" She is surprised and offended, and her emotional response becomes heated. Rather than trying to adopt a tone of reconciliation, question him about his misperception, or try to root out the "grudge" that is interfering with this mundane chore, she engages in an emotional confrontation that escalates to verbal combat because she now feels like the injured party who has been treated unfairly. He, on the other hand, perceives that he is the injured party who is owed an apology. Their perceptions, although different, lead them both to believe that the situation is skewed against them.

In the scheme of this particular theory, *perception*, the first aspect of marital harmony, relates to how we perceive events in our marriage through the lens of our past experience. When an individual is moved emotionally by something that's happening to them in the present, they are most likely to remember past events that triggered a similar mood. For example, in a distressing moment, unhappy spouses may recall negative events from their past in order to make sense of present conflicts in their marriage and to escalate the argument (Fincham, Bradbury, & Scott 1990). The more significant the past events and the more organized the individual's memory, the more likely one's current experiences will trigger particular memories. Thus, we are predisposed by our past to interpret or misinterpret our spouse based on our memories of similar emotional events. Similarly, we tend to make general assessments of our spouse and carry an overriding sentiment about him or her that filters out the meaning or intent of their immediate behavior (Weiss 1980). Finally, we observe each other with our eyes and ears, but we perceive each other based on the meaning we attribute to our observations. A wife might make breakfast for her husband every morning because it gives her joy to do so. A husband might perceive this generous gesture as her attempt to make up for all the hard work he does to support her. If he is predisposed (by events in his past) to be displeased with her, then he will misinterpret her actions in a negative way. (In 1980, Robinson and Price found that couples did not accurately remember or underreported the number of positive events in their daily lives and focused instead on the negative events.)

The *emotional response* aspect of this marital harmony theory has to do with how we react to our own and our partner's perceptions. When our perception differs from our mate's, do we take the time to sort out the key issues and work toward resolution, using our communication abilities? Or do we tend to get so emotionally worked up that we can't listen to the other person's point of view, can't stand to hear anything contrary to our own perception, and either veer off into verbal combat or withdraw in order to escape from the unbearable tension of arguing? If a partner feels unmoved emotionally, or expresses an intellectualized attitude toward a certain matter, he or she may attribute little importance to the issue or to their spouse in that moment. They may appear cold and dismissive, which may cause the spouse to feel abandoned. On the other hand, a partner may have very strong emotional responses to a particular event, which can overwhelm their spouse and cause him or her to withdraw for fear of escalating the discussion beyond their control.

The third aspect that affects marital harmony, according to Gottman, is the way we communicate and resolve conflicts. The way we communicate and resolve conflicts with each other influences how we perceive our relationship. Unfortunately, the longer a couple is married, the less flexible and the more fixed we become in the ways we relate to each other. The longer a couple is together, the more assumptions they have about each other. With growing familiarity, they tend to guess how the other will feel about something. If a couple is basically satisfied with each other, they tend to assume and expect the other's approval. However, if they are dissatisfied with each other, they tend to expect the other's disapproval. Thus, positive encounters reinforce more positive encounters, and vice versa.

This aspect of relating is a major focus of couples' counseling, where communication styles are analyzed and more satisfying methods of communicating are taught and practiced. To put it another way, we learn to replace silent, unworkable intuitions with functional ones (Lewis et al. 2002). This is described in more detail below.

John Gottman wrote, "Most problematic issues (69% in fact) don't get *solved*, they get *managed*. Positivity in interactions in happy couples is 20 to 1; in conflicted couples it is 5 to 1; and in soon-to-divorce couples it is 8 to 1. Watching a couple interact when they are *not* in conflict is the best way to predict their risk for divorce... Positivity means that there is a positive filter that alters how couples remember past events and view new issues."

According to Gottman, positivity is made up of a number of factors: (1) A *fondness and admiration system,* in which the couple is affectionate and clear about the things they value and admire in the other, (2) *love maps* or a good knowledge of the partner's world (work, family, self) and showing an interest in it during nonconflict times, (3) the *ability to survive conflict* by:

- *softened startups*, or tactful ways to bring up a problem
- staying calm during the argument so no one gets "emotionally overheated"
- *acceptance of influence*, so partners can accept the desires and wishes of their partners
- *repair attempts* or efforts to make up by using humor or conceding a point during an argument
- de-escalation of hot emotions and efforts to compromise
- *bids for affection* or efforts to connect through a shared joke, a quick kiss, or a quiet smile that is returned
- finding the underlying reason for the conflict and a way to meet both partners' needs

Gottman contrasts destructive conflicts as having these characteristics:

- Criticism—"What kind of person are you?"
- Contempt—"I would never be so low as to do something like *that*!"
- Defensiveness—"Yeah? Well what about what *you* did?"
- Stonewalling—Withdrawing and refusing to discuss the issue further. Rather than become outwardly emotional, a person might vent their emotions internally by thinking to themselves, "I can't believe she's saying this!"

When a couple disengages from constructive argument due to any of these reasons, Dr. Gottman predicts that they are likely headed for divorce within 12 or more years. In a destructive argument, where partners continually hammer each other with criticism, contempt, and defensiveness, the emotional distance between them increases as the argument continues. If a couple repeatedly reaches a gridlock over their issues, then Gottman predicts divorce in only 5 to 7 years. His guidelines for couples' therapy is designed to move from gridlock to dialogue; learn how to soothe each other in order to recover from an argument; and reconnect with each other by remembering those things that attracted you to each other in the first place.

Finally, Gottman teaches that when it comes to arguments, the *type* of person one partners with (attacker, soother, avoider) is not so important as the *mismatch* between the couple:

- soothers overwhelm avoiders, and you get the distancer-pursuer dynamic
- soothers and attackers have little ability to influence each other, little positive sentiment, and a great deal of emotional tension

- avoiders and attackers are the worst pairing, with a severe distancer-pursuer dynamic

In Appendices 1 and 2, you'll find two of John Gottman's marriage quizzes, which describe your personal *Love Map* and *Bids for Connection*. I recommend that you take these quizzes now so that you can assess the current strengths and weaknesses in your relationship.

ATTACHMENT THEORY OF MARITAL HARMONY

According to this theory, trust is the cornerstone of a relationship, and we learn to trust early. For some, it may seem hard to believe that the foundation of our personalities and the quality of our relationships is laid in our infancy. Yet, this is exactly what this theory proposes. As babies, we cry out when we're hungry or distressed. When our parent responds to us in a caring and consistent way, we learn that we can trust that person, that we are worthy of their love, and that by being close to that person we will be safe.

Some take this notion a step further. To a newborn baby who has no experience with the outside world and no way to distinguish between different objects or different people, their parent is their entire world. When a parent is trustworthy and caring, the baby learns that the world is a safe place as long as he can be with that parent. People who grow up with this positive early experience are said to have a *secure style of attachment*. Even in adulthood, they respond to distress by drawing closer to their intimate partners, because safety has always been found in the close proximity of those who care for them. According to Dr. M. Mikulincer, young adults who grew up in this way are "prone to forming close relationships, and would be particularly ready to search for intimacy and interdependence. They would put emphasis on the benefits of being together with a romantic partner, be more likely to dismiss potential relationship threats and wounds, and organize their goals around attaining and maintaining intimacy and closeness. In this way, attachment security would enhance a person's motivation to be involved in long-lasting stable couple relationship."

But what about those whose early childhood needs were not adequately met and who didn't form a secure attachment with their parent? When an infant cries out in distress and does not receive good-enough parenting, when their cries are ignored or their needs are not satisfied, they learn to distrust their caregiver and to be apprehensive in relating to the world. As an adult, when they approach another person, especially in an intimate relationship, they are extremely guarded; they do not assume that their cries for help will be met with goodwill. Their experiences with nonresponsive parents teach them that trying to get close to someone and trying to be loved is painful. They learn that they are unworthy and unlovable. Therefore, their goals and behaviors in relating to people are developed as defenses against the distress caused by their early attachment experiences (Bowlby 1988). These people are said to have *insecure styles of attachment*. Among the many categories of insecurity, we focus primarily on two types: those who are *avoidant* and those who are *anxious* in regard to relating to others.

Infants who receive care in an inconsistent fashion—sometimes it's there when they need it, sometimes it's not—develop an *anxious style of attachment*. As adults, they worry that others won't be there for them when they need them to be. When they're distressed, they reach out for closeness to others but do so in a clinging, needy way. They are hyper-vigilant for signs of security and affection but distrustful that they will receive what they need. Most commonly, such people feel frustrated, dissatisfied, and unloved. Sometimes, in a self-fulfilling prophecy, they create conditions that cause their partner to distance him/herself. Thus, their insatiable need for love and affection always seems unfilled, and they continue to feel insecure.

Some infants whose caregivers are not responsive to their needs develop a premature independence and avoid relying on others to satisfy their needs. Such persons are said to have an *avoidant style of attachment*. They distrust others, and in an effort to defend themselves against the pain of disappointment, they take steps to maintain their emotional distance. They search for autonomy and control and are reluctant to form interdependent relationships (Bowlby 1988). Often glorifying their self-sufficiency, they defend themselves against anticipated pain in relationships by disengaging their emotional need for others.

It is not news that these early infant-parent interactions affect us through adulthood and especially in marriage. In 1979, John Bowlby wrote, "There is a strong causal relationship between an individual's experiences with his parents and his later capacity to make emotional bonds." He highlighted marriage as the bond most likely to manifest the influence of early attachment.

In trying to understand our expectations of love and marriage, we can see their close connection to our earliest experiences of receiving care and comfort. Being secure means that we trust we will find comfort in the caring arms of our beloved. In the preverbal, intuitive language of the infant, we learned the endearing, nuanced, unspoken patterns of loving and comfort. Throughout our life, we may recognize those same patterns in others and feel drawn to them by "something in the way she moves me," something that is reminiscent of our earliest love.

Modern research in attachment theory is at the cutting edge of our understanding of successful relationships. From what we can glean at this time, imparting security to our children is a gift that benefits generations to come. *Securely attached* individuals are more likely to establish satisfying relationships, to successfully manage relationship problems, and to regulate their emotions so that they do not escalate out of control. Families that create a supportive home life facilitate secure mother-child and father-child relationships, and in turn the adult child's ability to love is enhanced. Securely attached individuals are more optimistic about love relationships and marriage, and often marry others who are also secure (Carnelley & Janoff-Bulman 1992; Pietromonaco & Carnelley 1994; Whitaker, Beach, Etherton, Wakefield, & Anderson 1999).

PERSONALITY SIMILARITIES THEORY

It turns out that opposites don't necessarily attract. Researchers at the University of Iowa found that people tend to marry those who are similar in attitudes, religion, and values. However, results show that couples with highly similar attitudes and values had little similarity in personality-related areas such as attachment, extraversion, conscientiousness, and positive or negative emotions. They found instead that *similarity in personality* seems more important in having a happy marriage. When they assessed marital quality and happiness, they found that personality similarity was related to marital satisfaction, but attitude similarity was not.

Why do some of us marry those with whom we have more in common attitude-wise than personality-wise? The researchers in Iowa found that, "People may be attracted to those who have similar attitudes, values, and beliefs and even marry them, at least in part, on the basis of this similarity because attitudes are highly visible and salient characteristics, and they are fundamental to the way people lead their lives." Personality-related characteristics, on the other hand, take much longer to be known and to be accurately perceived and are not likely to play a more substantial role until later in the relationship (Shanhong & Klohnen, 2005).

What do we mean by "personality?" We mean a person's way of relating to others and their general outlook on the world. Personality types describe the ways in which an individual consistently responds to the world around him. For example, a politician may be charismatic or obnoxious; acquaintances can be aggressive and competitive, submissive and quiescent, or supportive and collaborative; students can be compulsive or avoidant (procrastinators). One personality type might be dramatic and emotional, another overly rational, strict, fastidious, and stingy; another might be shy or introverted.

Do differences in personalities mean that your relationship is doomed? Of course not. Partners can have differing outlooks and ways of relating that nonetheless support and enhance their confidence and sense of wellbeing. We refer to such couples as "complementing each other." Complementary personalities can definitely have successful marriages. They may "fill-in the blanks" for each other and feel more competent when they're together. What the research suggests, though, is that there is a limit to how much difference can be tolerated in a marriage. A highly intellectual person may be attracted to a very emotionally expressive person, but in the long run they may interfere with more than complement each other. A prince may marry a showgirl (as in the classic Marilyn Monroe film) but may not feel supported when he takes her to visit the Queen, and she may feel like a fish out of water. A highly controlling personality matched with someone with a laissez-faire attitude may cause enough conflicts to splinter steel.

There are some personality types, however, that *require* differences in a mate. For example, someone who is organized and detail-oriented might dovetail beautifully with someone who values order but tends to focus on the bigger picture. He may be a terrific gourmet cook who knows just where to hunt down the best culinary specialties and how to organize the dinner party by planning the day before the big event; while she is the more outgoing, charismatic partner who is more concerned with making sure their guests have a good time. She appreciates being able to rely on a spouse who can take care of the culinary details, while she sees to the social relationships. And he appreciates being able to make his guests feel welcome in the way he knows best: cooking for them.

Another good pairing might be a down-to-earth pragmatist who excels at keeping her eye on the ball, and an adventurous risk-taker who revels in "going for it." The pragmatist might appreciate a partner who can help her take more chances in life, and the adventurer might appreciate someone who's more grounded and can balance his risk-taking tendencies.

Each of these couples has a chance to *complement* each other. They can rely on each other's strengths, defer to each other in the areas where they're less proficient, and trust each other to make things better for the two of them as a couple. If they are fortunate enough to succeed in life in the ways they wish to, they will share the credit with each other in a most genuine way. Two complementary collaborators who succeed together where each may have faltered on their own.

It takes time to know another's personality, to see if the differences between you will be constructive, destructive, or complementary. We may believe that our differences add spice to life, but that's true only up to a point. Some common ground is needed to be able to empathize with each other, see eye-to-eye, and gain enough understanding of each other to be able to manage differences in a satisfactory way.

In the Appendices, there are a number of personality-related questions that you can answer separately, in private and in writing, before sharing the answers with each other. Like all of the suggested questionnaires and exercises in this book, they were chosen to help you and your partner know each other better and sooner. They are not tests of personality, but they target key issues that might reveal similar, complementary, or differing attitudes and personalities. After you've finished reading this book, you and your partner are encouraged to take your time answering those questions. If your answers seem straightforward and support your goals as individuals and as a couple, you may feel encouraged to continue preparing for marriage on your own. If your answers seem provocative, you may want to include a marriage counselor in your pre-wedding conversations. He or she can help you sort out which differences you and your partner can adjust to and which you may not be able to so easily.

HOLMAN'S FOUR PREDICTORS OF MARITAL QUALITY AND STABILITY

In 2001, psychologist Thomas Holman published his comprehensive review of the research on predicting marital success and proposed a model that identified four broad premarital predictors of later marital quality and stability. He noted that these factors do not act independently but are interactive and strongly influence the effects of others. The factors are:

1. *Family Background*—Similarity of family background was found to contribute to a high level of marital adjustment only if both members of the couple came from emotionally healthy families. The opposite was also true: when both members of the couple came from emotionally unhealthy families, the lowest level of adjustment resulted. Also, for both men and women, closeness to fathers improved their marriages.
2. *Individual Characteristics*—These include personality, attitudes, beliefs, and values associated with relationships. Regarding gender differences, Holman noted that a female's positive perception of her physical attractiveness was related to her perception of the couple's communication quality, which in turn positively related to the male's readiness to marry. However, a male's sense of his physical attractiveness was unrelated to communication quality, but was directly and negatively related to his readiness to marry. In other words, a woman who feels she is attractive also feels more successful communicating with men, which encourages a man, in turn, to draw closer to her, often leading to marriage. A man who believes he is physically attractive does not necessarily perceive himself as a better communicator, and his physical attractiveness negatively impacts his readiness to marry.
3. *Couple Interactional Processes*—Generally speaking, the longer a couple knows one another before marriage the better. Premarital pregnancy was related to marital problems and not to satisfaction. In 1994, Holman noted that cohabitation was related to lower subsequent marriage quality. Regarding communication, "couples who could build consensus and who later constructed a shared view of the relationship ground rules had greater relationship quality."
4. *Current Social Context*—Holman stated that if a partner's race or gender is perceived by society to have a negative or controversial meaning, this could negatively affect marital satisfaction. For instance, an interracial

couple, a couple of mixed religious or ethnic backgrounds, or a same-sex couple might meet with disapproval due to prevailing cultural attitudes. Such couples might easily fit in within a liberal environment, but could be ostracized if they live in a more conservative one. We know from the research that such couples can survive quite well if they are satisfied within their own relationship. But they can be emotionally taxed by the problems that arise from their choices. To be prepared, the couple needs to anticipate the negative reactions from others and discuss how they can best deal with it together. Since the problem involves a societal outlook that the couple cannot control, they need to consider whether it is a potential threat to their relationship or something they can manage as a couple. In addition, Holman and his group of researchers noted that parental support is related to marital quality. Parental opposition was related to marital problems but not to marital satisfaction.

MARITAL RED FLAGS

According to Dr. Ted Huston of the University of Texas, changes in a couple's marital relations during the first 2 years of marriage foreshadow their relationship over the long-term. Huston followed his research couples for 13 years and found that the changes that took place in the first 2 years were still present after thirteen. What are the *red flags* that warn couples their marriage is likely in trouble? Huston lists the following:

- Disillusionment
- Feeling less love for each other
- Less physical affection between partners
- Less conviction that your spouse is responsive
- Increased ambivalence

In Huston's study, the couples that divorced within the first 2 years showed signs of disillusionment and were negative toward one another in the first 2 months of their marriage. Those who were disillusioned within the first year were likely to have trouble in their marriage. And those who had positive feelings about their spouse in the first 2 years were still happily married after 13 years.

According to Huston, the following are among the priority issues a couple needs to face the first year: how to allocate and handle money, who's going to do what chores, how to spend free time, finding time to have sex, dealing with in-laws, understanding differences including spirituality, learning how to deal with conflict, and *discussing expectations*.

It is sobering to consider potential *red flags* in your relationship when all you really want to do is joyfully walk down the aisle. However, it is important not to ignore them. As we've seen in the stories highlighted in this chapter, once the thrill of being in love subsides, couples experience a sense of loss. You may ask yourself, "Will our compatibility and love for each other be enough to sustain us once the blissful period ends? Without the initial thrill of being in love, does our relationship have enough of what we'll need to be satisfied and happy? Is our relationship "good enough" for us to commit to marriage?"

Like all the other questions we've asked in this chapter, these are vitally important. But even when the answers are not exactly what you might wish for, they are not reasons to be discouraged. If you feel a sense of disillusionment as you examine your expectations and the realities of life and love, it is likely the loss of a fantasy. The fantasy that your relationship—any relationship—can be perfect, and that you'll live happily ever after with no quarrels, misunderstandings, or tears. You can believe in that fantasy when you're focused on your similarities, but it bursts like a beautiful balloon when you consider your differences. Still, is a fantasy really what you want? If it can only be maintained by ignoring your partner's or your own individuality, how could it possibly survive in the real world, and how could it serve your own best interests?

This book is an opportunity to see how resilient your love is. You may find yourself falling more in love, becoming more confident in the love you and your partner share, once you know more about what it takes to make love last. Sometimes it may seem that love brings with it too many complications. Can those enrich you and make your life more fulfilling? Since life brings challenges and difficulties regardless of one's marital status, wouldn't you prefer to face them with your partner's help? Perhaps it is in marriage that we not only have the opportunity to love and appreciate someone else, but to more deeply know and love ourselves as well.

As you read through this final list of *marital red flags*, ask yourself, "How would I handle this if it happened to me? Could I handle it, or would it break me? Now I am a single person and can make choices that are best for *me*; once I marry, will I be able and willing to make choices that are best for *us*?"

Every marriage inevitably goes through normal ups and downs, especially in the first few years. By expecting such changes, you and your partner have the best chance to deal with them and get past them, together.

Marital Red Flags

- Lack of romance and intimacy
- Inability to have fun together
- Selfishness
- Fear of conflict
- Lack of respect
- Over-spending

- Over-dependence on parents
- Sexual problems
- Addictions and/or substance abuse
- Emotional and/or physical abuse
- Unrealistic expectations
- Over-commitment of time to activities that separate one spouse from the other. For example, a sports-loving spouse may never be available to his partner when the home team is playing a game. The nonsports fan partner thus feels rejected, as if she is a lower priority than the sports team. Similarly, one partner's overcommitment to work, even when it is in the service of the couple's financial welfare, may leave the other partner feeling abandoned.

None of these problems necessarily represents a threat to the marriage, but they need to be dealt with in a mutually acceptable way before they become one.

A "GOOD-ENOUGH MARRIAGE" SUCCESS STORY

It's hard to find a more controversial couple than Mary Matalin and James Carville, political advisors for opposing political parties. Carville ran President Clinton's campaign while Matalin ran President H.W. Bush's re-election campaign. These two are proof that opposites *do* attract. Opposites in political opinions but not in personality type, they set the newsroom on fire every time they appear on the Sunday morning news magazines. It's hard to find anyone more critical of one than the other. Yet, their marriage seems a great success.

The Carville-Matalin marriage shows us how resilient love can be and how one can separate the personal from the professional. Otherwise, how could they withstand each other's harsh professional criticism? "Both Carville and Matalin do an admirable job of maintaining their individual dignity and conjugal privacy," says the editor of their book *All's Fair*. After all these years, they're still together and fiery as ever. Theirs is an exemplary marital success story because, although their political perspectives couldn't be more different, their outspoken, dedicated, enthusiastic personalities seem to be a perfect match. They are witty, strategic professionals who share everything in common except the politicians they're fighting for.

In the film *Speechless*, loosely based on the lives of Carville and Matalin, the couple goes through a remarkable courtship during which the woman asks the man a question that was most important to her: What would you do if I slept with another person and then came to you and said it was a mistake and would never happen again? A previous lover had replied to the woman: I'd be hurt but I'd still love you, and I would hope we could get counseling to find out what's wrong with us that made you need him.

A sensible answer but wholly unsatisfactory to her. Her soon-to-be-spouse answered the same question in a funny but straightforward way: Infidelity is unforgivable and that would be the end of the marriage. That was the answer the heroine was looking for. Marital fidelity was a make-or-break issue, and they each felt safer with each other because they agreed on this point.

Like the happy couple in *Speechless*, even though we may differ on a range of issues with our partner, we need to be honest with them about our essential values and make sure they are on the same page.

RISING TO LOVE

They say that couples who make use of premarital counseling (which includes those of you who are reading this book) improve their chances for a lasting marriage by one third. Taking a serious look at your relationship is beneficial, enlightening—and challenging. The process brings to mind this passage, written in 1913, by Jack London. He wrote of his hillside vineyard in Glen Ellen, California:

> *I ride over my beautiful ranch. Between my legs is a beautiful horse. The air is wine. The grapes on a score of rolling hills are red with autumn flame. Across Sonoma Mountain, wisps of sea fog are stealing. The afternoon sun smolders in the drowsy sky. I have everything to make me glad I am alive ...*

For a pre-wed couple to counsel themselves so thoroughly and remain undaunted, even encouraged, by what they've learned, can be like drinking that wine. At this point in the book, much of the groundwork for a lasting marriage has been laid, so you are entitled to pause and appreciate—and celebrate—what you've achieved. It is a developmental milestone to know what is enough to make you glad to be alive. It is an even greater good fortune to find it in a partner who is happy to stay the course with you.

In the Chinese language, they say a couple *rises* to love rather than *falls* in love. Perhaps they're right. We rise to love, like rising to a great occasion, by being prepared and then trusting ourselves to do the right thing. In the next few chapters we'll continue our work. I hope it will continue to add confidence to your love and answer many of the questions you have.

Some of you may be stirred by what you've discovered about your relationship. I hope this experience can help you come to terms with whatever troubles you, so that you can rise to love more freely and happily.

Chapter 3

The Marriage Contract and the Prenuptial Agreement: Reflecting Your True Intentions

In this contract governed by the laws of the State, the couple exchanges vows to:

1. Love, honor, and cherish.
2. In sickness and in health.
3. For richer or for poorer.
4. Forsaking all others, be faithful only to each other.
5. Until death do us part.

These are the common vows of marriage, although they have been written in many different and poetic ways. "No matter what subtle differences there are in the wording of the ceremony, the spirit is the same. All of these words are steeped in rich traditions of the sacred message of a lasting bond" (Smith 2005).

We are steeped in the sacred. By this rite of passage, we change how all others see us and how we see ourselves. We do this out of a sense of *moral certainty, having no reasonable doubt* that our marriage is in the best interest of everyone.

This contract calls upon our highest sense of moral reasoning to abide by our vows. In so doing, we are expected to *govern ourselves* in regard to our moral behavior. We would not expect the State to *govern us* in matters of private moral behavior. In terms of statutory law, our adherence to our moral vows is not *legally enforceable*. That is, our vows of love, fidelity, and to remain together as long as we both live, are traditional or customary vows

(Parisi 1999). They are not enforceable under the laws of the State. One's behavior in regard to the vows is *morally persuasive*. In a court of law, it may persuade the Court to use its discretion when deciding other related issues. Other than that, injury to those vows is the source of a couple's differences, which are *reconcilable or irreconcilable*. Irreconcilable differences are the official cause of a dissolution of a marriage on moral grounds. It is a no-fault divorce and is the law in California and many other states. Except in cases where there has been abuse or criminal behavior, the content of a couple's differences is not of interest to the Court.

On the other hand, our vows to each other to remain together "in sickness and in health, for richer or for poorer" refer to our social security and community property, not to moral behavior or judgment. These vows are legally enforceable. It is the custom of the Court to decide in these matters by *Stare Decisis*—the doctrine of precedent, under which it is necessary for courts to follow earlier judicial decisions when the same points arise again in litigation. The custom of the Court does not directly stem from the same moral tradition that leads us to marry and does not always share the same common sense. Should any of these vows ever be contested, then we are accountable to ourselves in matters that are moral, and to the State in matters that are tangible and financial.

It seems ironic: our moral certainty that leads us to marry cannot be sheltered by this contract. At the same time, the contract binds us in financial matters that we are most naïve about before marriage and cause the most angst in divorce.

And a second irony: Most people have strong negative feelings about signing a *prenuptial* agreement, even though it can be used to govern oneself, within limits, by writing one's own enforceable vows. Yet, we eagerly enter into this *nuptial* agreement without fully understanding the laws of the State that bind us.

This marriage contract, which governs such a huge part of our lives, contains subtleties that can surprise us. With this in mind, let's take a closer look at the fine print.

MORAL REASONING AND PERSUASION

This contract calls upon our highest sense of moral reasoning to abide by our vows. In so doing, we are expected to *govern ourselves* in regard to our moral behavior. What is meant by our highest sense of moral reasoning?

In 1991, Lawrence Kohlberg and others developed and refined the stage theory of moral reasoning and development. The stages build on each other as we age, develop greater experience with moral issues and greater reasoning capacity. Each stage in moral reasoning is more complex than the one before. Therefore, moral decision-making is a developmental task that requires time and personal development both mentally and physically. It is believed that a majority of the population can reach stage 4 and a small percentage strives for stage 6.

Here are the stages of moral reasoning and growth that are characterized by the following behaviors:

- *Preconventional level* (stages 1 and 2): Behaving according to socially acceptable norms because they are told to do so by some authority figure (e.g., parent or teacher); believing that right behavior means acting in one's own best interests. Avoidance of punishment and obedience to parents or authority figures are the determining factors.
- *Conventional level* (stages 3 and 4): Behaving in order to gain the approval of others; abiding by the law and responding to the obligations of duty.
- *Postconventional level* (stages 5 and 6): The morality of self-accepted moral principles in which individuals voluntarily comply with rules on a basis of their ethical principles and make exceptions to rules in certain circumstances. Understanding social mutuality with a genuine interest in the welfare of others; respecting universal principles and the demands of individual conscience. (Fowers, Montel, & Olson 1996)

It is believed that a majority of the population can reach stage 4 and a small percentage strive for stage 6.

For Kohlberg, morality is chiefly a matter of relations between individuals. For other researchers such as Jurgen Habermas, it is chiefly a matter of a communal good; or Augusto Blasi, who thinks morality may involve such questions as our duties to God (Barger 1998).

By applying our highest level of moral reasoning we recognize our own ability to determine right from wrong. We accept most rules and laws out of a personal belief that they are in the best interest of ourselves and others.

1. We are not motivated to marry because we are obligated to do so (in fact, a shotgun wedding is in itself grounds for divorce. But separating under such intense pressure, like having a shotgun to your head, can be very difficult).
2. We do not marry in order to gain the approval of others (although social sanctions reinforce a marriage, and the approval of others is a primary factor in marital success).
3. We usually do not marry in order to avoid punishment, although some couples with special needs or compromising situations may avoid punishment, such as being socially ostracized, by marrying.
4. Some people argue that there should be punishment in the form of greater civil penalties for divorce, and those penalties should act as a deterrent to divorce. Given the high divorce rate and the inherent punishment one suffers by going through a divorce, adding penalties seems

to be an ineffective deterrent. What we know about punishment from learning theory and forensic studies is this: in order for it to be effective, punishment must be immediate, unavoidable, and of adequate valence to get a person's attention. By these criteria, divorce as a punishment can never be an effective deterrent to a marriage failing. The implication is that there is something *in* a failing marriage that is more immediate, more unavoidable, more noxious, more *punishing* than the duress of divorce.

For people using their highest level of moral reasoning, the wedding vows are deeply felt, personally meaningful, and consciously assumed. One does not need the threat of punishment, the rules of convention, or the fear of lost prestige to marry and stay married. It is within their imagination to be a part of a couple and to thrive in marriage's safe haven.

In Appendix 3, there is a brief questionnaire that helps you determine your own current level of moral reasoning. When it is convenient, I recommend you take a moment with that questionnaire and see where you stand on this scale. As with all of the resources presented here, these are offered for your own information. There are no right or wrong answers, and your answers are confidential: you needn't share the results with anyone. Therefore, be honest; answer according to how you feel at this moment. You might learn something useful about yourself, including how you compare on that scale to your own self-image at this moment.

To return to an earlier point, "It is believed that a majority of the population can reach stage 4 and a small percentage strive for stage 6." At stage 4 we play by the rules. If the rules of social convention are adequate for a couple, then they enjoy great independence within society. The couple has an adequate model of acceptable moral behavior; they know how to treat each other in marriage because they see how others do it and accept that as healthy and normal. They do not need greater guidance or restrictions from society, nor do they feel unduly constrained by social convention.

When one at any level of reasoning needs, wants, or believes that he benefits from guidance in morality, then we often find comfort in our religious traditions. In many historical, orthodox religions, a detailed code of moral conduct is handed down. In this way, higher moral reasoning may be achieved by proxy, from a higher moral authority. We have a way laid out before us and that is reassuring. We rely on the authority of our personal moral leaders that the code is righteous and fair and worthy of reverence. For people who value a traditional religion, the orthodoxy serves a great social function: It organizes both society and the individual, and provides a place where we can socialize with others of like-mind. In return, we are held accountable for our wedding vows to that moral authority in whom we are personally invested.

This is worth looking at closely for a number of reasons. First, most premarital counseling is offered by the church or clergy (because it is convenient and usually free). One should know what the church expects before you say "I do." Also, what help is available when you need it, and what are the consequences if things go wrong? Most books published on premarital counseling take a religious approach, often a Christian approach, to marriage. One should know what assumptions are being made so you are free to accept them knowingly. One should understand how the moral authority enforces the wedding vows, just as one should know how the State enforces "that which is Caesar's." For these reasons, I draw an example from a once strict but now moderate religious tradition.

The Catholic Church in the United States

In the United States, the Catholic Church has traditionally intervened to exhort consciences, propose values, and describe moral behavior. It has used its authority in marriages to hold almost inviolable the fifth vow "Until death do us part" by forbidding divorce or annulment except under special and rare situations. In recent years, however, their attitudes and practices have been changing.

This is happening within the context of a great social upheaval, where the Courts are testing the legitimacy of interventions by moral or secular bodies in a person's civil rights. These tests are occurring around the world, with secular groups from many traditions, in the Courts, at the Embassies, and on the streets. The Pope has recognized this in his encyclical on moral theology, "Certain currents of modern thought exalt freedom to such an extent that it becomes an absolute, which would then be the source of values. The traditional doctrine is rejected; certain of the Church's moral teachings are found simply unacceptable; and the Magisterium itself is considered capable of intervening in matters of morality only in order to 'exhort consciences' and to 'propose values,' in the light of which each individual will independently make his or her decisions and life choices."

Clearly, there are those within the Church that oppose these currents of modern thought. "There can be no doubt that this situation in the modern Conciliar Church of Pope John XXIII's Vatican II has been and continues to be *a grave scandal*, and that, once again, the true Church of Christ, the Catholic Church, is publicly discredited by this Conciliar Church" (Bishop Mark A. Pivarunas, CMRI, October 7, 1997).

What is the grave scandal the Bishop is referring to? It is the Church's attitude toward marriage and divorce. The Bishop continues, "In recent months the news media has focused its attention on the extremely high number of marriage annulments which are annually granted by the modern Catholic Church, especially in the United States. An annulment is an official declaration by the Catholic Church that a marriage is invalid—that is, not a true marriage—from its very inception. There are a number of reasons that a marriage can be proved invalid. Among them are lack of canonical form, induced grave and unjust force or fear, diriment impediments, and lack of intention in regard to the primary purpose of marriage—that is, procreation of children—and to the essential properties of marriage—that is, indissolubility and unity."

Since the advent of Vatican Council II, the number of annulments in the United States has escalated to a phenomenal proportion. Why, may we ask, has this taken place? "Ever since the Church began recognizing psychological grounds for annulments in 1970, there's been an absolute explosion in their number" (Zwach 1983).

Prior to Vatican II, the only psychological grounds accepted for annulments were those in which one of the parties to the marriage did not possess the use of reason as to be incapable of a human act of the will to consent to the marriage contract.

The official numbers of annulments in the United States since the Second Vatican Council are as follows:

1984—36,461

1985—53,320

1987—60,570

1988—50,000

1989—61,416

1990—62,824

Let us compare the numbers above with the 392 annulments granted by the Catholic Church *worldwide* for all the years between 1952 and 1956.

We can recall the marriage statistics of Traditional Couples, who may be represented in the above statistics. Those couples enjoyed the greatest longevity in their marriage, but also represented 50 percent of married couples who were "less-happy." When an unhappy, traditional couple no longer faces opposition from the church, then they no longer face the moral dilemma or the risk of being socially ostracized by divorce. Their social context is changed; the amount of unhappiness they are expected to endure is lowered. For some, that threshold may be lowered enough to take that step toward annulment or divorce. The Bishop finds it scandalous that such personal freedoms should take precedence over the original intention of marriage, "til death do you part." But now, it is for each of us to decide where our values lie.

In his book *Inside: A Public and Private Life*, Joseph A. Califano Jr. wrote, "I have often thought about the stigma attached to annulments: that they were granted only to the biggest donors or most famous members of the church. Still, I took notice in 1997 when Sheila Rauch Kennedy published a scalding book, *Shattered Faith*, about the annulment of her marriage to Massachusetts Congressman Joseph P. Kennedy II. She recounts a conversation in which she says she will oppose the annulment, and Joe Kennedy responds, "I don't believe this stuff. Nobody actually believes it. It's just Catholic gobbledygook, Sheila. But you just have to say it this way because, well, because that's the way the church is."

How common is this sentiment, one wonders. Belief may not be demonstrated by the above statistics, but compliance and commitment to the Church's moral and social authority is. People who marry under a religious canopy place value there. Apparently, *they continue to place value there when they seek healing by means of annulment.*

For those who want to read more about the Church's moral reasoning regarding annulment and a revised and *morally enforceable* Code of Canon Law, they are reprinted in Appendix 4 and enumerate the psychological grounds for annulment.

LEGAL REASONING AND ENFORCEMENT

Partners often talk about who wears the pants in the family. When it comes to the wedding contract, the conversation is almost the same: Who controls the terms of marriage; the husband and wife, or the State?

The main issue here is control. Many researchers have discovered that control is a key issue in marital success (along with a couple's closeness). If the State dictates the terms of your marriage, do you agree to those terms? If not, are you informed enough about your options to take control and write your own nuptial contract? You may be so eager to *be* married that you can't wait to sign on the dotted line. But are you, by virtue of your thorough understanding of what marriage means, *of Sound Mind* to enter into this contract?

When engaged couples discuss the law, they take control of their marriage. It can be difficult to discuss because it is only tested in divorce, which is already unthinkable. Also because it focuses on the financial aspect of marriage, which is so unromantic.

The State has no such qualms and has established detailed guidelines for the Court to follow. It has also established a power of wide discretion for Judges to determine what is fair and equitable. Couples should not assume that the State's rendition of what is fair jibes with their own common sense. When a couple enters into this Nuptial Agreement, they are submitting to the State's authority to govern them.

When you discuss finances with your fiancé(e), the focus is on your plans to achieve some wealth and security. Your spouse is your partner; your business partner whom you trust. With his or her help, you can work toward goals you might never aspire to on your own. It can only strengthen a partnership to start with a sound business plan.

The reality is that most couples have not made financial plan. Most have not taken the first step to formulate a plan by writing a monthly budget for themselves (Fowers and Olson 1992). In fact, most couples do not even broach the subject of finances until 2 months after the wedding (Dubin 2001). Does anyone see a red flag flying?

Couples who have not prepared for financial realities give control to the State by default. Now, a couple may be satisfied by the State's provisions for them. You may accept the social convention, in which case there is no problem. However, if you are not informed of those provisions and accept them anyway, or if you prefer self-governance but do not take steps to write your own marriage contract, then you start your marriage in a one-down position: you are *not* in control.

Although this may be tested only in divorce, our attitudes toward each other and the value we assign to each other *during marriage* are largely determined by these laws.

For example, we may assume that "equal partners" in a marriage means that everything is shared 50:50. According to the law in many states, however, discretion is given to the Court to decide if one spouse is entitled to 50 percent of the estate or as little as 30 percent. Are you a 50 percent partner or a 30 percent partner? Does this definition of equality jibe with your own common sense? Are you comfortable submitting such an important decision to a Court, knowing that its discretion may go against you?

A second example: In the vow to remain faithful in sickness and in health, we are directed to take responsibility for our health insurance, retirement resources, and our wellness and physical fitness. This provision causes concern for everyone, married couples and legislators alike, because our system of social security is not secure. It may be a problem that is ultimately managed but not solved. Still, we are obligated to apply due diligence to provide for our own needs and future needs. Our legislators caution us against trusting the Social Security System to provide for all our needs in retirement, which "was designed only to be a safety net, not a carry-all for old age."

Control is the main issue here. You may decide to take control or not, but hopefully your decision will be well-informed. Hopefully, you will make your decision based on a shared sense of personal *resolve. There is* no need to make a *commitment* to an external expectation when you can *resolve* to behave according to the married couple's best interest based on your own sense of moral certainty.

In order to be better informed, let's look at the three Great Contracts that we sign in our lifetime. They are:

The Marriage Contract,

The Last Will and Testament, and

The Prenuptial Agreement.

Surprised by the third? Did you expect maybe your mortgage or business loan to take third place? The surprise is just beginning.

Look at it this way: Of these three contracts, which has the greatest ability to trump the others in determining your estate plan? The prenuptial agreement. Which contract gives the individual the greatest power to determine how your property is managed *and* which laws govern its management? The prenup. Which contract best facilitates a conversation about property, finances, and lifestyle, looks to the future, and assures both partners that they will be treated fairly in the eyes of the law? Once again, it's the prenup. When we marry without a prenuptial agreement, we are agreeing to the state's system to decide what is equitable. When we write a prenuptial agreement, we are effectively writing our own vows that state what we mean by "equal" in terms of tangible assets.

Although the prenuptial agreement offers so much, it remains the contract least-often signed. The mere mention of a prenup causes hackles to rise, red flags to fan in the wind, and pre-weds to doubt the sincerity and commitment of each other. When one partner raises the issue, it can feel like he is already planning to divorce! The stigma attached to this contract is hard to overcome.

After a long talk about money, you may decide that you don't need a prenuptial agreement. But by having the discussion, you ward off a source of conflict that leads to 70 percent of modern divorces.

Also, this is not a one-shot deal: There is more than one opportunity to sign a prenup; it need not be signed before marriage. More and more married couples are writing *postnuptial agreements*, or *internuptial agreements*, that provide the same advantages in settling your estate plan. Like one's Last Will and Testament, it can be revised through the years as the need arises.

There are some important technicalities to observe. For example, these three contracts must be written with consistency, so they do not contradict each other. Otherwise, a contest might arise that could render one of the contracts invalid. Therefore, do-it-yourselfers are advised to have a professional check their work before signing.

Financial advisors recommend that couples have this talk 6 months before they marry. If you decide to sign a prenup, then it should be signed and sealed *before* the wedding invitations go out. Imagine the relief of having this premarital task behind you, versus the anxiety of finding potential problems in your relationship after the wedding gifts start to arrive.

It is beyond the scope of this book to describe the nuances of a prenuptial agreement. For continued reading, I highly recommend *Prenups for Lovers: A Romantic Guide to Prenuptial Agreements* by Arlene G. Dubin. The book is easy to read, comprehensive in scope, and sensitive to people's feelings about the topic. If you still need more personalized feedback about finances, then it is available from your premarital counselor, accountant, and attorney.

OF SOUND MIND

I am but mad north-north-west: when the wind is southerly I know a hawk from a handsaw.

—William Shakespeare

When we remember we are all mad, the mysteries disappear and life stands explained.

—Mark Twain

In The Last Will and Testament, one's final wishes are traditionally begun with the phrase:

I, *being of sound mind* and body, declare that this is my will.

To understand what soundness of mind means to the marriage contract, let's look at how it is measured in a will. After all, in some cases being fit to marry is predicated on one's soundness of mind to write a will.

In writing a will, a person is deemed to be of sound mind if he:

1. knows that he is writing a will and the purpose of his will,
2. knows the extent of his property, and
3. knows the beneficiaries of his estate.

These criteria are easy to prove, especially at the time the will is written. Some individuals who wish to prove that they are of sound mind (and thus avoid an ugly scene between beneficiaries in probate court) use a psychologist to conduct an Evaluation of Testamentary Capacity. The psychologist interviews the individual, sometimes on videotape, asks pertinent questions, corroborates his findings with third parties, and then makes a clinical judgment regarding his soundness of mind. The psychologist is then available to testify in Court should the need arise.

What criteria need to be satisfied in order for us to be of sound mind to marry? I have not found specific criteria written for this purpose. If we follow the same format as in the will, perhaps they would look like this:

In signing a marriage contract, a person is deemed to be of sound mind if he:

1. Knows he is getting married, the purpose of the marriage contract, the nature of the marriage ceremony, and the obligations and responsibilities of the marriage.
2. Knows the extent of his property that will be affected by the marriage (which is everything you own or jointly own now and in the future).
3. Knows who he is marrying and is clear about his relationship with her.

In other words, if one has the mental capacity to know, the freedom to choose, knowledge of his fiancée, and the nature of marriage, then he is fit to sign a marriage contract and be bound by it.

Unless someone is objecting to the marriage, the State assumes that an individual meets the first two criteria.

Regarding one's knowledge of one's self and fiancée, it is the purpose of this book and every premarital counseling program to inform engaged couples in a personal way *so they will be of sound mind to marry*. By now, you have already invested some time reading this book, and there are still a few things to discuss.

Let's take a brief look at some of the counseling programs offered to see what the experts believe it takes to bring a couple up to speed on the fine points of marriage. A more thorough review of resources for couples can be found in Chapter 9.

Loyola College of Maryland described their program, or Pre-Cana preparation, which is designed to gain an appreciation of the rights and obligations of marriage:

> Beginning a marriage is perhaps the most important step that people take in their lives. It is an event for which life often prepares us poorly. While love is the foundation of marriage, love alone cannot be our only preparation for marriage, for married life may be difficult and may feel "less-than-loving," at times. The Church cares deeply for couples entering the Sacrament of Marriage and offers these Pre-Cana sessions as part of the preparation for your life together. Pre-Cana is 9-12 hours in length. Married volunteer leader couples, trained by the Archdiocese, facilitate the sessions, drawing from and sharing with you experiences from their own marriage in the areas of communication, decision-making/finances, human sexuality, and marital spirituality. You'll be asked to listen to presentations on these topics, to do written exercises from a workbook, to participate in small-group discussions and to engage in personal sharing with your future spouse.

Programs vary in regard to the depth and details of marriage that are covered. Most premarital counseling programs meet for 4–6 sessions and may spend roughly the same amount of time, 9–12 hours, together. In private counseling with a psychologist, one may expect to spend about the same amount of time. Couple retreats and weekend workshops can be more time intensive, but lack the time between sessions for the couple to consider and digest what's been said.

These programs range in cost from free to members of a congregation, to some hundreds of dollars for a psychological consult. This compares very favorably to the high cost of divorce. For example, in a high-conflict divorce where child custody is in dispute, a psychological evaluation that makes recommendations for placement of the child(ren) with one parent or the other costs at least $7,000. That does not include attorneys' fees and court costs. And little is learned during these evaluations that couldn't be learned in premarital counseling, with much less expense and heartache.

The main reason to attend some form of premarital counseling goes back to our discussion in Chapter 1. If you are in love, then you are likely in an altered mental state. It may not seem like love interferes with judgment because it feels good. Everything makes sense as far as one can see. Psychologists would say the mood is "egosyntonic," that is, love makes sense to us. It organizes us in a wonderful way. But the delicate balance of reason is easily tipped in the direction of one's preference when influenced by intuition or strong emotions.

"When two people are under the influence of the most violent, most insane, most delusive, and most transient of passions, they are required to swear that they will remain in that excited, abnormal, and exhausting condition continuously until death do them part" (G.B. Shaw, *Getting Married*, 1908).

Compare this to the old saying "don't make decisions in anger." In anger, one is aroused but not in a way that feels good. In anger, one may not care about what's best. In anger, we often feel injured and frustrated. A common impulse is to "get what's fair" which means to get what's mine, what should be mine, or to get even. Thus, in the altered state of anger, a foolish decision may seem fair in the heat of the moment.

Being in an altered state of love won't prevent you from driving a car or signing a contract, but it may indicate the need to get a third party's opinion. Listening to a counselor may change an unseen opportunity for regret into a confident anticipation of a satisfying married life. Counselors can make this offer by using all of their resources; their clinical expertise and the use of psychological assessment, which is discussed in Chapter 9.

This discussion wouldn't be complete without looking at some of the ways a marriage contract won't work. Some of the examples are comical, some are sad. Hopefully, none of these things will happen to *you*.

INVALID MARRIAGE CONTRACTS

There are ways that a marriage can be voided. Some of these may seem fair to you, others may not. But this is where we stand at the moment, according to the laws in most States:

- The couple is same sex
- One partner is already married
- One partner lacks mental capacity or is insane (not responsible for his actions due to mental health reasons)

- One partner is underaged
- One partner is drunk at time of marriage (this may affect a lot of us, but it probably applies to the stereotypical last-minute Las Vegas wedding or to the couple in the first example below)
- The relationship is within the prohibited degrees of conduct, as in the second example below

Till Death Do Us Part . . . Or Until the End of the Wedding Reception At Least

This marriage, which lasted for all of 90 minutes after a whirlwind engagement of only 8 weeks, has been billed as the world's least successful marriage.

When Scott, 23, and Victoria, 39, tied the knot last week, they like all newlyweds were looking forward to a lifetime of wedded bliss together. And as the two lovebirds left the church and headed off to a "top-hat and tails" reception, no one could have guessed that within 90 minutes, the loving couple would be filing for divorce on the grounds of irreconcilable differences!

Apparently, things took a turn for the worse when Scott, who according to friends, had been "drinking like a Russian fish," staggered to his feet and began to drunkenly toast the bridesmaids.

According to witnesses, Scott behaved "disgracefully" and his "toast" apparently consisted of him swaying about on top of the table, sloshed out of his mind on ale, while screaming suggestive comments at some of the female guests.

This was all too much for new wife Vicky, who leapt into action and struck Scott over the head with a heavy ashtray in an attempt to subdue him (or possibly kill him!). The stunned guests watched in horror and then ran for cover as an enraged Scott grabbed a hat-stand and threw it javelin-style at a large mirror behind the bar.

Police were called to the scene but had to abandon their attempts to calm Scott down as he head-butted one officer and punched another in the eye before being dragged to jail, at which point Vicky cancelled their honeymoon and began divorce proceedings. (©2004–2005 The Gag Report™)

Child Bride's Husband Sent to Prison

A 23-year-old man was sentenced to more than a year in prison on a sexual assault charge filed after he impregnated a teenager, then married her last spring when she was 14.

Judge Daniel Bryan sentenced Matthew Koso to 18 to 30 months in prison, saying probation wasn't an option because Koso continued to have sexual relations with his underage wife.

"Marriage is one of our most sacred institutions," Bryan said, "and it appeared to be the answer in this case, but it can't cover up a crime, and it can't make it go away."

Koso and the girl legally married in Kansas in May, after the teen's mother gave the couple permission. Kansas does not have a minimum age as long as there is parental or judicial consent; Nebraska requires those getting married to be at least 17.

Crystal Koso, now 15, urged the judge to be lenient, saying she loved her husband and wanted her daughter, born August 24, to have a chance to know him. "If you send my husband to jail, maybe you'll see my daughter here in 15 years," she said. The couple cried together as Koso was sentenced.

Nebraska Attorney General Jon Bruning made headlines when he charged Koso last summer. He said his office had an obligation to protect children in Nebraska, where state law prohibits people 19 or older from having sex with those under 16.

The case prompted Kansas officials to introduce a bill banning marriage for anyone 15 and under and preserving the requirement for parental or judicial consent for those aged 16 or 17. (February 7, 2006, Falls City, Nebraska [AP])

Finally, there are ways that a person can attack the validity of a marriage:

- Mental Competency: The person attacking the validity of the marriage must prove that a spouse was incapable of understanding the nature of the relationship and the obligations and responsibilities it involves.
- Testamentary Capacity: When a marriage is challenged due to circumstances that reflect on the mental capacity of the testator to make a will, the person seeking to uphold the marriage must prove his competency. In other words, if you are capable of signing a will, then you are capable of getting married. (However, a lack of testamentary capacity is not in itself determinative of capacity to marry.)
- Capacity to Give a Power of Attorney for Property: The attorney is probably responsible to demonstrate one's inability to assign this power.
- Undue Influence: The person alleging that he or she was coerced into marriage (by an angry relative with a shotgun, for example) must prove coercion. (Rose, Gonin, & Sammon, 1998)

In cases where any of these conditions may apply, then one is advised to seek legal counsel. In all things, get the help you need to be prepared for marriage.

By planning ahead, this marriage contract may be a bridge, and not a fence, between us.

Chapter 4

How Marriage Will Change You—For Better or for Worse

It is not the strongest of the species that survives, nor the most intelligent, but the most responsive to change.

—Charles Darwin, 1859

Women hope men will change after marriage but they don't; men hope women won't change but they do.

—Bettina Arndt, 1986

The wedding is over, now it's just you two. Some couples were fortunate to take a honeymoon vacation, some had to go right back to work, or child rearing, or moving house. The thank you notes still need to go out (those important little things that let the people who have always loved you know you care). You might want time to debrief with your bridesmaids and best man. You might need time to recover from all the wedding planning. And even though everything turned out fine, you might need some time for just a little melancholy from the post-wedding-day blues.

This is a busy time. Once the dust settles and things start getting back to normal, newlyweds start to notice that what used to be normal isn't normal anymore. It is not entirely unexpected. For the most part, it can be the best of times; "They dream in courtship, but in wedlock wake" (Alexander Pope, 1713). But adjusting to a new spouse's habits requires effort. As Robert Anderson said, "In every marriage more than a week old, there are grounds for divorce. The trick is to find, and continue to find, grounds for marriage." We know from earlier research that married couples who are able to establish a routine and a consensus about rules of the house within the first year are off to a very good start, especially if their new routine includes private time for themselves.

I have often heard that there is one time in a person's week that is most intimate, most valuable. For some it's an evening off together with nothing to do, for others it is the morning of their day off. Love happens in discreet moments, even though married couples are bound forever. In the wedding ceremony, it is said that the ring symbolizes love with no beginning or end. Surely, time spent in love is a timeless moment, purely subjective, when one is completely absorbed in the moment. It might be the feeling of really connecting for those few minutes, when your attention was undivided from your spouse that sustains you for the whole week. Observe them. Keep them alive. Those Saturday or Sunday mornings when you feel the greatest need to be drowsy and unhurried, to crunch your pillow one extra time, to find your beloved there beside you and move closer so you both notice, without needing to say, that you fit. Or drowse off together again and nap, or love before breakfast, or snap-off the sheets and let's go biking, or just a most heartfelt good morning, and on with the day, glazed with the predisposition of comfort and connection and tolerance.

Taking time for love creates the condition for love to thrive. Establishing a household routine is necessary to get through a well-managed day. But this is not the core issue driving postnuptial adjustment.

At the heart of the change that newlyweds experience is the maturing and development of the dream of love. From a dream built together, there slowly emerges a dream awakened, laced with the diversity of two individuals. Newlyweds get acquainted without the powerful influence of courtship or the constant positive reinforcement lauded on them by friends and family. The dream divides, matures, individuates, and love must change to accommodate. What was once jointly created in a charged atmosphere is now challenged by a shared life made up of individual contributions. The dream is pulled and tugged by each partner's distinct vision of it. We all have individual needs, one of which is to remain an individual in this new family. This is healthy, this is normal. This is also the time when arguments and discord begin.

If courtship and early marriage is the infancy of love, then the time of adjustment after marriage is the "terrible twos." Spouses learn to say "no" to each other. Each tries to assert his independence, guided and limited by mutual respect and affection. The challenge of living with someone who is truly your equal may be the greatest adjustment of all. For many, this may be the first time in their lives where they have been in an equal partnership with another. There is no roadmap here, and negotiations need to be carried out frequently and with all the diplomacy one can muster. This can be an exciting phase of growth. Projects and responsibilities that were beyond the ability of a single person become possible for a cooperative couple. It can also be a frustrating time when each's effort interferes with the other's. In this new climate, spouses try to reconcile the early dream of love with the reality of marriage.

Earlier chapters have emphasized the importance of conflict resolution and assertive communication in successful marriages. There are two other aspects of communication worth noting. First, the use of humor. If the argument of the day is not really so serious, lighten up about it. This doesn't mean one has to disengage from a quarrel about a relatively trivial thing, only to keep it in perspective. It doesn't mean one can disregard all the advice on how to fight fair either, although some people like Phyllis Diller make a joke out of that, too: "Never go to bed mad. Stay up and fight" she advises. It is healthy and normal for couples to disagree. "The concept of two people living together for 25 years without a serious dispute suggests a lack of spirit only to be admired in sheep" (A.P. Herbert).

The second perspective comes again from Donald Winnicott who wrote about the constructive use of anger. Anger, he said, is our usual reaction to encounters with the Reality Principle which states that our gratification must often be delayed. Adults and kids are the same in this regard: we want what we want Now! When one has to wait, he can get frustrated and angry. But anger also surfaces in a healthy developmental way: When one has an idea about somebody being good and loving, how does he know for sure that this person is that way? How does he know that he hasn't misjudged her. How does he test it?

By surviving an argument together. When one voices a grievance to his spouse and an argument ensues, there is the potential for conciliation or for annihilation. We can agree to something, agree to disagree about something, find a compromise, or we can go nuclear and never speak to each other again. We marry someone who, one hopes, can negotiate the first three options without needing to resort to the fourth. Someone with the inclination and ability to tolerate two people's differences, have compassion for another's point of view, and maintain a basic level of respect and affection even in the face of adversity. We marry someone who is emotionally reliable and constant.

When the dream of love is first born, it originates from one person's imagination. One imagines love is this way or that, a partner is this way or that. In courtship, the belief and the feeling is that this dream is shared. To doubt one's belief in something imaginary is not negative in any way. The doubt need not be conscious for one to want to verify it, to get a reality check: Is my partner truly that way? What would happen if something came between us? Would she still treat me the same, would she still love me?

In an argument, we have a chance to find out. If a couple survives an argument and can get back on the same page with each other, then there is evidence that one's perception of love and partner is not strictly imaginary.

That is, she really is loving and reasonable and respectful. We might not agree on whatever we argued about, but she engaged me respectfully, and I won't be afraid or avoidant when I need to confront her again. In this way, the imaginary spouse is destroyed in favor of the creation of the real-life spouse.

There is tremendous satisfaction in surviving an argument. People often report feeling unexpectedly happy and relieved to survive their first battle, their first threat of annihilation. As a result, they trust their partner more because they have witnessed the other in adversity and found her to be constant, and control could be shared. There is less to fear because the couple feels free to differ without destroying the relationship. What attracts people to each other is their compatibility. What defines resilience in a marriage is how they deal with incompatibility.

The dream of love need not be lost when the honeymoon is over, but it must grow and develop. Resiliency allows a marriage to grow. Inflexibility, rigid thinking and behavior freeze the dream in its infancy, where it can remain fixated like a fish in a too-small aquarium, either squirming and straining to grow, or complacent with its condition in the company of love's imposter. Or it can burst out under pressure, sometimes inappropriately. It is the difference between an argument being reconcilable or irreconcilable. To the success of a marriage, it makes all the difference in the world.

When spouses' expectations of each other are rational and genial, then there is a great opportunity for love to do its best: What is different about us makes us curious, what is complementary about us gives us comfort, what is the same about us gives us strength.

CHANGE FOR BETTER

On Conversation

Wilfred Bion compared conversation to breathing. You take in fresh air, mix it up inside you, and return it changed by the way you processed it. It's a very intimate connection, conversation. It is a very personal sharing that happens when two people can take turns just hearing each other, and then returning it with a bit of yourself added. Much more than sex, this kind of intimate connection sustains happily married couples; a vital treasure to the marriage as it moves on in years. The great intensity of emotions at the beginning of a relationship is hard to maintain, seductive and wonderful as it is. True conversation is necessary to be intimate, to stay connected with the special qualities of the person you married. For example, here is an excerpt from *West Running Brook* by Robert Frost:

> 'Fred, where is north?
> 'North? North is there, my love.
> The brook runs west.'
> 'West-running Brook then call it.'
> (West-Running Brook men call it to this day.)

"The Conversation," Edouard Manet (1832–1833). Courtesy Erich Lessing/Art Resource, NY.

'What does it think it's doing running west
When all the other country brooks flow east
To reach the ocean? It must be the brook
Can trust itself to go by contraries
The way I can with you — and you with me—
Because we're — we're — I don't know what we are.
What are we?'
'Young or new?'
'We must be something.'
                         * * *
'It is this backward motion toward the source,
Against the stream, that most we see ourselves in,
 The tribute of the current to the source.
It is from this in nature we are from.
It is most us.'
'To-day will be the day. . . . You said so.'
'No, to-day will be the day
You said the brook was called West-running Brook.'
'To-day will be the day of what we both said.'

This is a beautiful conversation to me. Both are caring and attentive, interested in sharing and learning about each other, and finding their life reflected in the best of things.

Conversation can easily be waylaid in a host of ways. What we assume in a *true* conversation is mutual respect, the capacity and interest to listen, to consider, to respond. These underpinnings are essential to a stable platform for conversation. We often assume they are there in an intimate relationship, but they must not be taken for granted at risk of great peril. Without a conducive emotional climate, the conditions necessary for conversation are not there, and we start shooting from the hip in the style we grew accustomed to before marriage.

Conversation can be waylaid by our own passion, our own intensity of emotion that we treasure and gives us such pleasure. Intensity of emotions are so seductive. In courtship, it's the passion that sweeps us off our feet and overwhelmingly drives us to marry. It's all good in courtship. But in the course of a marriage when there is a conflict, intensity and passion reverse valence. Hot turns to cold unless spouses can reach a meeting of the minds through conversation and thus regulate their feelings and keep things within tolerable limits. Without the rudder of intimacy, intense love turns into intense rage. Emotions reverse themselves and sometimes the jibe is hard. It is not uncommon that the same passion that first attracted one to a partner ultimately causes their separation.

For example, this first statement from a young wife, still flushed from her wedding day:

> ...I hope that we still feel like newlyweds no matter how long we are together. Maybe we have to cultivate it. Maybe if we get to be oldly wed we should go do something radical so we can be newly again. Radical like take a retreat, hike a mountain, take a vacation, buy a house, complete a project, share an altered consciousness, take a dance class, repeat our first date, try a different position, learn a new technique, sail a boat....
> I love you
> My friend, lover, husband.

The same wife, some short time later after an unsuccessfully managed argument, vents her final frustration with the same intensity of emotion but with an opposite valence:

> You are now trying to make it seem as if it is my fault.
> You are Despicable!
> Your attorney can contact my attorney.
> We will have to let the law settle our financial matters but you still have to
>   live with yourself!

The reversal can happen gradually or with remarkable speed, with real *and* imagined projections of blame and shame unless there is some inner regulation of our emotions to moderate our responses and hold firmly to the common goal: to hear and be heard on the way to resolve and reconciliation. Without that rudder, intimate partners are apt to target with unconscious precision the sensitive issues that can challenge the relationship.

Conversations can be waylaid by disengagement, loss of interest or intimacy, or by fitting into a role so completely that one's individuality is consumed by it. This happens often in couples who organize their marriage based on traditional roles, or on power and control. The vicissitudes of marriage are too many to list. The hope is that one has a clear sense of the goal—open conversation—and can navigate the challenges as they arise and get help or mediation when needed.

Marriage needs a constant conscious effort to choose what is best for one's spouse, what is best for *us*, even before deciding what would be best for you. There is so much to consider. A healthy marriage needs input; bids from each spouse as often as possible to stay connected and inject fun and interest into the day. It requires the maintenance of soundness of mind, not only to decide to marry but to maintain a healthy and growing relationship.

A woman still happily married after 34 years put her experience this way:

> When asked how I adjust to a long-term relationship, the word "adjust" seems too static to me. The interface between me and my husband/partner of 34 years is constantly evolving. We are two very different individuals who respect and admire each other . . . to a point (!), and share some basic life goals.
>
> You put 2 people together, be it partners, parent/child, or pretty much any situation, and over time all the basic human flaws and idiosyncrasies float to the surface. The question then is how you respond to them. The endearing becomes annoying or commonplace, things you hoped were temporary you realize are not only permanent but getting more extreme.
>
> My experience is it's a learn-as-you-go. And it seems the biggest, most ferocious issues have the most obvious solutions. It's the little stuff that sucks the joy out of life. So the puzzle is how to deal with the big stuff and handle the little stuff so it doesn't drive you to distraction. I know that the small stuff is so many copper pennies and the good stuff is gold, and to try not to give anything more value than it deserves. And I have learned that humor is disarming, and that all of us, in all our stubborn and opinionated beliefs are really just speculating.
>
> How I have evolved within any relationship has everything to do with me and just a little to do with my partner. Over time I have come to recognize things which have created personal boundaries and limitations as well as greater tolerance and understanding.

I know that I must stand up for things that are life-path important to me. I am an individual and when something is core to my beliefs I do it. I must. What I suffer by surrendering entirely who I am is 100 times worse than the suffering caused by disagreement. It is my partner's call whether he can accept it or not. And I have learned conversely that I am in no position to challenge his life-path objectives as well. The trick is learning to recognize them in both of us and that it is a never ending work in progress.

After many years of relationship and the raising of 3 children to adulthood, I FINALLY realized that the reason they all vent at me while being delightful to the rest of the world is that they feel safe with me. And when I freak out at it, it is a betrayal to myself as well as to their trust. It has been the hardest thing to accept that I am not the cause, the fault, or even the trigger of the other person's distress—my response may be the most liberating.

The type of person I am is probably disgustingly optimistic. I am endlessly curious, amazed, and astounded by the possibilities in almost every moment. Life is a challenge in the best of ways, and there are countless ways to experience it. When I am awake enough to remember it is my choice how to experience any particular moment I choose to embrace it. What could possibly be a better alternative? (Dottie Hochberg-Simmons)

CHANGE FOR WORSE

When a couple's expectations of each other are not shared, or do not seem rational or genial to each other, when arguments lead to escalation and resentment instead of resolution and confidence, then one may need to examine the assumptions underlying the argument to see where this difference gathers such impetus.

"People marry for a variety of reasons...One person may look to the spouse to meet unfulfilled childhood needs for good parenting. Another may see the spouse as someone to be saved from an otherwise unhappy life. Irrational expectations between spouses increase the risk of marital problems. How a marriage works out relates to the partners selected, the personality organization or disorganization of each, the interaction between them, and the original reasons for the union" (Kaplan & Sadock 2007, p. 49).

When the dream of love is in its infancy, it has only one dreamer who is in control. In reality there are at least two people in control of the dream and how it plays out. In the above example, the couple was able to moderate their control and their need for it, and came to an equitable solution. When two people marry in order to satisfy "unfulfilled needs for good parenting" or to "save another from an otherwise unhappy life," then discord develops:

the role of a spouse and the individual's personality become incompatible with the expectation. A husband cannot be a father, a wife cannot be a mother. No one can be the other's therapist. A spouse who wishes it were so cannot himself be a child again, who needed to receive those things during a *critical period* in his childhood. Critical period, meaning that satisfaction of one's needs are time sensitive. He either got what he needed at that time or it was too late. If those needs are unfulfilled, then they are lost to him. They cannot be satisfied. They can be grieved in the company of someone with compassion for your grief. However, when we try to get satisfaction from a spouse for needs that are unsatisfiable, disillusionment sets in. Buddhists refer to this condition as the *"Realm of the Hungry Ghosts"*:

> The hungry ghost state arises out of the cold hell. You eventually have to relax from the position of being frozen, or of maintaining rigidity. You relax because you can no longer relate to how you are maintaining your rigidity. But then you freeze, because you dare not move lest you provoke that ever-escalating intensity again. You don't venture into any other fields of experience that present themselves, because they all look like pain. So you freeze everything in order to survive. You maintain the tension of that frozen state by refusing to move even if there's a good possibility that some situation might be preferable. You don't move into it because you've learnt that freezing keeps you safe. Naturally it's an effort to remain frozen, because opportunities are always arising. The enlightened state is always flashing through, even in hell! And whenever this happens one has the opportunity to respond—to move or cooperate with it. When you relax in that sense of opportunity, something new always opens up. It always starts out feeling like a big risk. But when you first sense that there is some opportunity that seems more nurturing, you enter into the hungry ghost realm. You taste something different and become very hungry for positive experience. The problem is that it's a completely self-obsessed state. You have no interest or respect for what you're going for; you just want to devour things. Because there's no basic respect for what is being devoured, there's no compassion in the relationship with it. When there is no compassion in your relationship with phenomena, whatever you devour turns into poison. Whatever you drink turns into something disgusting; traditionally you'd say it turned into liquid fire. This is the kind of analogy that's given of the hungry ghost, the yidag. The yidag is a being with a huge mouth and a very thin neck. It can get a lot into its mouth but it can't swallow anything. Whatever it sees looks good, so it eats it—but then it always turns out to be bad. It turns out to be really vile! It turns out to be bad because of how it's crammed into the mouth. It's a little bit like going to some amazing restaurant where the food is wonderful but you slather all over the table cloth and dribble on the waiter's arm. Then when the meal arrives you stuff it into your mouth so fast that you choke on

it. No matter how tasty it was, it would cause you pain because that's what happens when you turn into some kind of human vacuum cleaner. You can't possibly swallow food as quickly as you'd like to swallow it. There's so much in your mouth that you can't swallow, but you can't take it out either, because you're starving. So this is the quality of being a yidag. (http://www.aroter.org/articles/6realms.htm)

A person who is starving for nurturing that is no longer available often tries to satisfy that hunger with substitutes: wealth, prestige, ownership. This behavior is often accompanied by a sense of entitlement to those things, without regard for the reality principle or the welfare of others. There may be a sense that, once marriage is consummated, it no longer requires the effort made in courtship to maintain it. As one takes control of oneself in the marriage, the role and power assigned to the other may be determined by one's internal images from the past; the role that other's have played at different times in your life. A spouse is unable to speak to a partner who sees him as father, ex-husband, or perpetrator. He needs a third party to make communication possible. If such feelings surface in the course of a marriage then it could best be addressed with a psychologist. These issues can be worked through with a competent therapist, a patient and persistently supportive spouse, and the individual who uses the resources that are available in the present to grow and break free of bonds from the past, in order *to forsake all others.*

Regarding Kaplan's second citation about those who see their spouse as someone to be saved from an otherwise unhappy life. He is referring to the rescue fantasy, the Pretty Woman fantasy, etc. I guess we see it happen often enough in life and cinema that we believe it could happen to us; we could win the jackpot. But after the rescue, then what; they lived happily ever after? They could, if the jackpot were *enough* to satisfy all the needs created from a probably traumatic rescue. Second, if the rescue was successful and returned the survivor to a prior, high-functioning condition. Third, if the rescuer wasn't counting on a scripted response from his rescued. If, if, if. The chances of meeting criteria to satisfy an irrational expectation are small. There are so many possible reasons that people marry—someone to talk to, someone to take care of my children, someone who will make me special just by being with me, etc.—and it would be in the best interest of the marriage to talk about them, make them known if you can.

Reasons to marry are not always expressed to the spouse before or even during marriage. Still, when one feels secure enough in the relationship to let his true feelings show, the spouse is expected to respond in a way that supports those reasons and needs. However, when such hungry ghosts dominate the interactions of spouses, then they can pull the living relationship right out of present and back to the past.

This recalls the earlier argument about the kind of partnership we enter into in marriage: equal partners, traditional partners. Partners who are faithful to each other by paying attention to each other in the present, and are not unfaithful to their partner by letting the suffering of the past take control of the present, which is now shared.

Chapter 5

How Having Kids Will Affect Your Marriage

Newlyweds, new parents, and new children. There are 10,000 conversations people love to have about raising kids the right way. There are 10,000 chances to discuss not only how much one wants to get pregnant, but also how to raise a child that is wanted and cared for throughout childhood. And there are 10,000 rewards for taking the job as parent.

Will it change you or your marriage to have children? One expectant grandmother put it this way:

> We are sitting at lunch one day when my daughter casually mentions that she and her husband are thinking of starting a family.
>
> "We're taking a survey," she said half-joking. "Do you think I should have a baby?"

"It will change your life," I say, carefully keeping my tone neutral.

"I know," she says, "no more sleeping in on weekends, no more spontaneous vacations."

But that is not what I meant at all. I look at my daughter, trying to decide what to tell her. I want her to know what she will never learn in childbirth classes. I want to tell her the physical wounds of childbearing will heal, but becoming a mother will leave her with an emotional wound so raw that she will be forever vulnerable.

I consider warning her that she will never again read a newspaper without asking, "What if that had been My child?" That every plane crash, every house fire will haunt her. That when she sees pictures of starving children, she will wonder if there could be anything worse than watching your child die. I look at her carefully manicured nails and stylish suit and think that no matter how sophisticated she is, becoming a mother will reduce her to the primitive level of a bear protecting her cub. That an urgent call of "Mom!" will cause her to drop a soufflé or her best crystal without a moment's hesitation. I feel that I should warn her that no matter how many years she has invested in her career, she will be professionally derailed by motherhood. She might arrange for childcare, but one day she will be going into an important business meeting and she will think of her baby's sweet smell. She will have to use every ounce of discipline to keep from running home, just to make sure her baby is alright.

I want my daughter to know that everyday decisions will no longer be routine. That a 5-year-old boy's desire to go to the men's room rather than the women's at McDonald's will become a major dilemma. That right there, in the midst of clattering trays and screaming children, issues of independence and gender identity will be weighed against the prospect that a child molester may be lurking in that restroom. However decisive she may be at the office, she will second-guess herself constantly as a mother.

Looking at my attractive daughter, I want to assure her that eventually she will shed the pounds of pregnancy, but she will never feel the same about herself. That her life, now so important, will be of less value to her once she has a child. That she would give up her life in a moment to save her offspring, but will also begin to hope for more years, not to accomplish her own dreams, but to watch her children accomplish theirs. I want her to know that a caesarian scar or shiny stretch marks will become badges of honor.

My daughter's relationship with her husband will change, but not in the way she thinks. I wish she could know just how much more you can love a man who is careful to powder the baby or who never hesitates to play with his child. I think she should know that she will fall in love with him again for reasons she would now find very unromantic.

I wish my daughter could sense the bond she will feel with women throughout history who have tried to stop war, prejudice and drunk driving.

I hope she will understand why I can think rationally about most issues, but become temporarily insane when I discuss the threat of nuclear war to my children's future. I want to describe to my daughter the exhilaration of seeing your child learn to ride a bike. I want to capture for her the belly laugh of a baby who is touching the soft fur of a dog or cat for the first time. I want her to taste the joy that is so real it actually hurts.

My daughter's quizzical look makes me realize that tears have formed in my eyes. "You'll never regret it," I finally say. Then I reached across the table, squeezed my daughter's hand and offered a silent prayer for her, and for me, and for all the mere mortal women who stumble their way into this most wonderful of callings.

And if we need a *father's* point of view, consider this:

If children come with nothing but worries and problems, why would people keep having them? As a father of five who was very willing to have more, I believe I can speak to the subject.

When I was presented with my first child, I felt like a heavy weight had been placed on my shoulders. She was blue with cold; I asked them to put her in the nursery. My only concern was for my wife and child's safety. That passed in a few moments when I saw they were ok. Then I felt like everything was right with the world. With the birth of my first grandchild, I felt like I'd done the most wonderful thing. I wanted to go to the top of the hospital, to the roof, and shout to the world *look at us*. We've done the most wonderful thing possible.

Nature has placed within us emotional rewards that are beyond belief. My most profound rewards have come from watching the children grow. The first rolling over, the first sitting up, the first word become milestones remembered for all time. Holding them, their soft warmth, feeding them, playing with them. The end of being lonely, the fun of being busy, the joy of marriage, and the pleasure of a thanks dad, or my dad can do anything, or please help me dad.

Once we took a trip to the beach. I swam into the water and dove through a breaking wave making a "hole in the ocean," as my daughter would say. A small thing, but she said that day she saw her father could do anything. I have more real pleasure from that day than from anything I have done in my professional life. Professional accomplishments are expected, but impressing your child is a thrilling thing.

In old age, who is there for you if not your children? I've seen others who have no family and believe me, it is no pleasure to be alone. All of the accumulated money and rewards from society cannot satisfy your needs. But your children, grandchildren, and great grandchildren do. It's just built in, naturally. Children are the ticket to a new world of responsibility, accomplishment, and joy.

So, the short answer to the question "will having children change my marriage?" is most definitely *Yes*. Like most prospective parents, you hope the change will be wonderful for your child, your spouse, and for yourself. It's easy to get caught up in the concerns of parenthood—will we be able to afford a child, will we have a healthy child, will we have a boy or a girl, how will the in-laws react? Will they help, and babysit on occasion, or at least offer their blessing?

One can relax a bit knowing that parenting skills (or step-parenting skills) need only be good-enough, not perfect, for a child to thrive. Perhaps the greatest thing we do is to share our time with them, focus on their needs, and try to model what you would like them to become. A healthy child is shaped by what he sees us do. Children model themselves on us. They learn more from what we do than from what we say. Our modeling becomes their central imago, the basis for their own sense of self, how they relate to others, and how they will parent their own children. We are their archetype for parenting, and we are the gatekeepers of the influences we have had from our own past.

Many people, especially expectant grandparents, urge newlyweds to have children as soon as possible. They have their own interests to consider, such as their own loudly ticking biological clocks. One hopeful father-in-law took his son-in-law out for an afternoon and actually drilled him on how to spell "baby" and "marriage." The son was hesitant to marry for very good reasons that were personal and related to his own best interest. But his prospective father-in-law liked him enough, saw that his daughter had chosen him to be her husband (although they had not set a date for the wedding) and wanted to hurry things along. "Shit or get off the pot" was his tactful way of telling him to get busy making babies. The son was clever enough to turn the conversation to his own advantage. He said, "Timing is everything. I don't sit down until I'm ready to do my business. Then you can be sure that I'll get things done, and they'll be well done." The father had to be satisfied with that, at least for now. He respected the son for thinking for himself. If the son could stand up to the pressure *he* brought to bear, then later he would be able to stand up for his daughter when they felt pressure from others. He didn't get his grandchild when he wanted one, but he did gain more respect for the son.

Another prospective mother-in-law who, in her own life, had maintained a career while keeping house and raising her children, coached her son in the opposite direction. "After you're married, date your wife for a while. Enjoy being a couple; enjoy being able to sleep together wherever you want, to do whatever you want. When you're ready for children, then you can have them; you have plenty of time. But once you have kids, your private time will be very limited. I know you'll be a wonderful father once you set your mind to it. Take your time now to enjoy just being a couple. You might not have this chance again until your children are grown and out of the house."

Both parents-in-law spoke with their best intentions. They were right to encourage children in their own ways: research shows that couples in a family way derive 66 percent of their satisfaction in life from their families. Yet, there is a growing number of couples who make the argument against having children. For example, The Future Foundation recently polled couples with qualities similar to the readers of this book that showed that that several factors will cause a couple to delay having children, or even reject the role of parenting altogether. Among those reasons, the change of lifestyle of the parents was especially potent. Half of males and 40 percent of females questioned believed they needed to change their lifestyle before having children. "We are participating in nearly double the amount of leisure activities which we did 25 years ago and having children would mean, more so than ever before, the willingness to slow down. Where lifestyle has the most impact is for those who have decided not to have children at all—"just deciding not to" or "not willing to change my lifestyle accounts for half of these decisions. . . . People are deciding to have children more as a lifestyle than a lifestage."

Long gone is the belief that "all you need is love." Finances are the greatest inhibitor to starting a family. Sixty-six percent of young married couples delay having children in order to build up their financial status, and 57 percent delay to afford a bigger home. Seven percent choose not to parent at all for this very reason!

Fear for the child's well-being is normal enough. The Future Foundation discovered that, although over a fifth of those surveyed were concerned about living in a dangerous neighborhood, 11 percent of potential parents believe the world is just not a safe enough place to raise children, and 7 percent fear that they would not be a good parent (The Future Foundation, August 2006).

For those who have children, they are becoming more reliant on grandparents and family (and, of course, a supportive spouse) to provide childcare because they *are trustworthy* and relieve the anxiety of sending the children to less-controlled care centers. For this reason, young parents are best helped by living closer to their own parents or in-laws.

In his book *Responsible Parenthood*, Dr. Gil Kliman discussed how we are not only responsible for teaching children, but also for *how* we teach them. We can choose what to transmit from our own upbringing, the noble or the insidious, by becoming aware of those influences and remaining vigilant about the practice of positive parenting (Kliman & Rosenfeld 1980).

Our parenting style, the match we make with our children, and our attunement with our family resonates and permeates everything we do at home. Life at home can be "all for one and one for all," celebrating together when we can, supporting and lending resilience when we must. Or, it can lead us vulnerable to unfortunate events for which we may not be prepared.

We have many chances to talk about how to raise kids the right way, but we have fewer chances to talk about what can go wrong. In most premarital counseling, couples are rarely asked about their own histories of hardship or abuse. If they *are* asked and there *has* been some unfortunate event in the past, then those couples are usually referred to someone like me for more in-depth counseling. Most programs are not prepared to discuss the consequences of having a difficult upbringing and how it might affect your marriage, your style of parenting, and your children. Therefore, there is a risk that these couples who most need counseling and support will not receive it from traditional premarital counseling.

I see the risk in the clinic everyday: the after-effects of child abuse, abused kids growing up and not knowing how to parent their own children, kids bouncing in foster care, good parents guilty of failing to protect their children and then losing them. Sometimes life does not prepare us well for parenting. This is especially true if we have special needs, like the need for extra help at home or at school, or with healthcare. No wonder 7 percent of the couples surveyed were afraid to have children of their own.

Then, there are those families that are beyond at-risk: families who have developed the need for others to step in and take control either in hospital or in prison. Kids are great, kids are the bees knees, but sometimes they test a parent's patience. Sometimes, something in a parent just "snaps," something goes wrong, and something bad happens. How it "snapped" says a lot about the person who snapped it. That it snapped at all means that the family's future just changed, and the kids are in the other room talking to a social worker.

Let's take this opportunity, for one chapter, to discuss the real problems that can happen in childrearing; to review what can go wrong. The mainstream population hears very little about the abuse that is epidemic in our society except when there is a headline about a particular case. By listing the types of abuse children suffer here, parents can be more prepared for the task ahead and avoid these pitfalls.

Perhaps a new wedding vow can be added "I shall not abuse my children or suffer them to be abused." It sounds odd to consider such a vow. It does not seem too much to ask, but do we really need such a vow?

Consider domestic violence. It is rare for experts to agree on one point, but in this there is complete agreement: In raising children, the best predictor of their negative development is exposure to *domestic violence* (Benjamin & Gollan 2003). This fundamental observation is memorized by experts who testify in child-custody disputes and is seriously considered by the Court in making decisions regarding child custody. This implies that *exposure to chronic domestic violence is more harmful than exposure to divorce*. Kids exposed to domestic violence, such as parents always arguing and fighting, or alcohol and substance abuse or worse, grow up scared and angry. They form the anxious attachments we talked about in Chapter 2. They may grow up believing that violence is the normal way for parents to behave. They may look for a spouse to punish them as one parent was punished. Or they may grow up identifying with the aggressor; finding it in themselves to punish others before they punish you. Children who grow up in violent homes often suffer anxiety, depression, and other mental health disorders as adults that are resistant to treatment. In extreme examples, Dr. Peter Fonagy discussed how the long-term effects of domestic violence can lead to boys growing up to be perpetrators of violence against women. He concluded that the best treatment for this type of psychological disturbance is primary prevention: to break the cycle of violence before it starts (Fonagy 1999).

Here, in premarital counseling, is the first best chance to guard against the transmission of domestic violence.

There are four main categories of child abuse to be aware of: sexual, physical, emotional, and neglect.

Regarding *sexual misconduct*, can we agree without long discussion that it is not ok to have sex with kids? Apparently not, since most children who are sexually abused are abused by an adult whom they know (Russell 1983; Wyatt 1985; Siegel et al. 1987; Sedlak & Broadhurst 1996). Parents who have been exposed to abuse may be more vulnerable to have abuse in their homes. They also have this opportunity to be strong gatekeepers against transmission of sexual abuse.

Regarding *physical violence*, we are referring to something beyond the usual discipline techniques. What form of discipline is acceptable to a couple? Potential parents should discuss their attitudes toward corporal punishment. Is there a place for it at all? Are times-out enough? Do we both discipline the kids or is one parent The Enforcer? In the old days, the "rule of thumb" meant that one could not beat a child (or a spouse) with a stick of wood wider than his thumb. Now, it is considered physical abuse if corporal punishment leaves a bruise or a scar. While corporal punishment is still widely practiced, research indicates that it is not the most effective deterrent to negative behavior in children because it can make the child more aggressive. The parent may become the inadvertent model of aggressive behavior, and/or the child may feel the need to transfer the aggression he's experienced to a smaller or younger child.

When a couple agrees that spanking is ok, or times-out are preferred, or grounding a child or rewarding a child in certain ways is best, then they can present a *United Parental Front* to the children and support each other when they need to set limits on the children. While the children still won't like to be disciplined, they are spared the confusion that results from parent's disagreement. Their argument over what "mom said, what dad said" is preempted by the parent's consideration of this issue in advance.

Regarding our special population of the young soldiers returning from the war, about one in six war zone veterans suffer from PTSD, or Posttraumatic Stress Disorder. Suffering this diagnosis raises their risk for domestic violence, according to the National Center for PTSD. Children of war zone veterans, particularly those raised by veterans with PTSD, are more likely than their peers to be aggressive and violent, to use drugs and alcohol, and to attempt suicide. The military is proactive in this field, quickly instituting programs to address this concern. The hope is that participants will be *amenable* to the program and get something of personal value out of it.

Also under the category of physical abuse is the violence done to a child before birth, when the pregnant mother exposes the child *in utero* to alcohol and drugs. According to Dr. Ann Streissguth, director of the Fetal Alcohol and Drug Unit at University of Washington:

> *Fetal Alcohol Syndrome (FAS) is an irreversible neurological disorder that is 100% preventable. FAS is associated with cognitive and developmental disorders that affect an individual over the entire lifespan. To prevent even the chance of contracting this disorder, can parents agree to abstain from using any drugs or alcohol during the course of pregnancy?*

Nine to ten months of abstinence does not seem too high a price to pay for a neurologically intact child.

Neglect is the silent perpetrator of domestic violence, which can be either benign or severe.

Benign: The unintentional, episodic or single episode of abuse: "I just left my baby in the car for a second, I didn't think it was so hot!" In this well-publicized example, the consequences of benign neglect can still be severe or even fatal.

Severe: Intentional or habitual neglect. For an in-depth example of severe neglect and domestic violence, I refer the reader to view the movie *Once Were Warriors*. The violence portrayed is horrific, but it is made easier to watch—and to learn from—because it has a hopeful ending.

Couples considering parenthood can discuss how active and involved they each intend to be in parenting. Do you each intend to help with homework, with rides to extracurricular events? What forms of discipline do you plan to practice? What about family vacations and special time for a child with one parent or the other? Is it important to you to take the family to church every Sunday? Does it matter to you if the kids play unsupervised, without curfew, without censor? These are very personal preferences that can only be decided by the parents. Although couples considering adoption need to complete a full battery of tests and questionnaires before they are allowed to adopt a child, no such screening or education is required of natural birth parents. No one can dictate how someone will raise their own children.

In having this discussion, consider if your guiding principle is the best interest of the child. This means that, at some time in the future, the best interest or the convenience of the parents will be sacrificed for the benefit of the child. This remarkable self-sacrifice may be more than a young couple can willingly take on. If so, then how long does the couple want to wait before starting a family and committing to such a sacrifice? The freedom, energy, and money dedicated to children are enormous. We cannot overestimate the amount a parent gives up in order to benefit a child.

Emotional abuse is the most controversial form of abuse and perhaps the most harmful of all. When a child is inappropriately exposed to parent's loud arguments, slamming doors, breaking dishes, veiled or overt threats, they are victims of domestic violence. Children are unable to fix problems that aren't theirs. They can't soothe themselves when they need to be soothed or shout "stop" with the hope of being heard. They are able to feel afraid, and too often they feel hopeless. Children that grow up afraid may be fearful their whole lives. Their feelings and behavior as adults may be centered on avoiding something fearful, or recklessly trying to prove to themselves that they are not afraid.

Does this mean that parents can't argue or disagree in front of the kids? Certainly not. Happily married couples argue. When they can do it respectfully and assertively, they model assertive communication for the children. When parents show their feelings but still let reason reign, then they model for their children that adults have feelings too, that their feelings won't destroy them, and that problems can be managed if not resolved.

This is easier said than done. We all have our soft spots; points that cause us to lose control. Even then, when one feels like lashing out or creating an opportunity for regret, there is a chance to model mature behavior for the children. When a parent takes time-out from an argument and agrees to come back to it later, after tempers have cooled a bit, they model this behavior for their children. Sometimes it seems that the main difference between a child and an adult is that adults can give themselves a time-out, while children still need help.

Kids listen to everything. They pay attention to adult conversations. Sometimes they can repeat them word for word. Sometimes, they interpret conversations in surprising ways. We need to be cautious about the signals we give the children. This is, after all, the model they will use for their own adult relationships in the future.

There is a useful guideline for communicating with children about parental disagreements. It comes from child custody evaluations drafted at the University of Washington. "Each parent is responsible for providing age-appropriate explanations to the child. The absence of negative

Courtesy Ten Speed Press.

communication is insufficient. It is expected that each parent will convey an optimistic appraisal when discussing [the issue.]"

Partners who bring children to a marriage face yet another set of challenges—the beginning of a new and unique relationship with each member of the family. A new stepparent may be meeting a stepchild who has already reached teenage years and whose mind and personality is already set. Or you may meet a younger child who reaches out for attention from a new stepparent and welcomes it when offered. Remember, the children get to know their stepparents during courtship, while their parents are still in this mind-altered state of love. The kids may have some romantic fantasies of their parents' marriage of their own. Their hopes are high, or alternately they don't dare to be high. Becoming a blended family takes time and consistency, so each person can learn to trust each other. It doesn't happen overnight. Even for those who have been cohabiting for some time, after you marry, changes come to your relationship with each person in your family just as surely as you change your name to husband, wife, son, and daughter.

One important and often overlooked consideration to stepparenting is how the biological mother or father will influence your life. Will he/she be active and present during the daily course of childrearing? Will you be able to establish some kind of rapport? Whether the biological parent is physically present or not, his or her influence on the children is constant and poignant. In children's minds, their natural parent is always present, for better and for worse.

Hopefully, parents can interact with each other in an amicable way. If, however, the step- and biological parents have trouble relating to each other for any reason, then it may be wise to set limits on the relationship. For example, conversations between parents could be limited to the immediate needs of the children: transportation to and from visits, sharing information about scheduled appointments, etc. They need not be friends in a general sense, but they do need to cooperate in order to serve the best interest of the children. In the next chapter, the story of Jerry and Lisa illustrates what can happen when the influence of parents competes instead of cooperates.

There are two final things to consider when blending a family: First, "When do I introduce my boy/girlfriend to my kids?" This is a very good question. Some parents won't introduce a potential partner until they feel secure in the new relationship. Many choose not to share too much about their dating until the children "need to know." Even then, introductions to a potential stepparent can be difficult and may benefit from some advanced planning. Should we tell them together or apart? Do we have answers for the questions we know they'll ask, like: Will we be changing schools? What about my real mom/dad. Does this mean I have to listen to Him? The couple can discuss what to tell the children and how they should be told. First impressions mean a lot, and this one couldn't mean more.

Second, in the sad and unhoped for event that your new marriage doesn't work out and you decide to separate or divorce, "How do we tell the kids?" As heartbreaking as it is for adults to separate, it can be no easier on the children. I'm afraid there are no good answers to this question, only choices of what's best and honest and least painful. If this time comes, then I recommend that you remember how you first agreed to introduce your fiancée in the beginning. If possible, I recommend that you repeat the process during your separation. The kids will react, and they may not be so diplomatic as you might hope. After all, this separation is a loss for them that they do not control. Try not to cut them off or make it impossible for them to communicate with you. Try not to alienate them from your estranged spouse or prevent them from saying goodbye. Make every effort to shield them from whatever poison surfaced between you in your engagement or marriage. Let them have their say. Whether you agree or not, whether it is fair or not, children need to be able to speak their minds without fear of retaliation.

They may have something to say, now or later, and the same goes for you. There is a chance that time may heal the wound if you can remain available to talk it out. Without the openness to have this conversation, there is a chance that time will only make the wound fester.

In an earlier chapter, we discussed prenuptial agreements and how they can help with separation. If you are considering writing a prenup, also consider adding a provision for some kind of counseling, discussion, or mediation with the children. Making an early arrangement to protect the children's feelings about separation could really help if it comes to it. At least, the children would know that you thought of them and their feelings matter to you. Even in this worst case scenario, there is a way to show caring and respect.

Chapter 6

Marrying the In-Laws

They say you date a person but marry their family. But when you marry a family without even dating, is it any surprise that problems arise? Look at all the expectations of our spouse we talked about in Chapter 2. Parents-in-law may have most of those expectations too. They stem, in general, from parents wanting the new spouse to be responsible to their grown child: to care for him/her, to be responsible as a husband/wife and parent, and "to make my son/daughter happy." Plus, parents carry expectations from their different cultures, times, and traditions. Where most traditional European and Western cultures expect newlyweds to be responsible to each other, other cultures, such as traditional Chinese or Japanese, expect newlyweds to fulfill specific roles in the hierarchy of their extended family. As intercultural marriages increase, we need to work harder to understand the "foreign customs" of our fiancée's family. Do you know what your new in-laws expect of you?

And one more consideration: How important to you are their expectations? Are your future parents-in-law present, are they an active part of your life? One might think that their living presence makes them more influential, more of a daily impact in your lives. But even when parents are absent they can still be very influential, by being often on your spouse's mind.

In the 1967 film classic *Guess Who's Coming to Dinner*, a young Caucasian girl brings her fiancée, a young and brilliant doctor, home to meet her liberally minded parents. The parents are challenged because, despite his impeccable credentials, he's African American in a time when interracial marriages were hardly ever seen or talked about. To make matters worse, the parents had not been alerted to the "surprise," and had only one day to decide to give their blessing or not.

Early in the evening, Sidney Poitier, playing the young doctor, says to his fiancée's father that he knows the odds are stacked against them and that they're choosing a difficult life for themselves. They love each other and want to spend their lives making each other happy. But he needs to have the father's approval. Without that, they would encounter hostility outside and no support inside their home. That would be unbearable, he said, and it would be better for all concerned if he called the wedding off.

The father, played by Spencer Tracy in his final role, ultimately gives an impassioned speech to the young couple about the struggles they will face and the unkindness that will be heaped on them, but that if they truly love each they will survive. And if that's truly what they want for each other, *then why was his opinion so important to them, anyway?*

Sometimes when there are children from a previous marriage involved, it's not the opinion of the parent-in-law that matters as much as the opinion of the previous spouse. Such was the case when Jerry wanted to marry Lisa, who had four children from a previous marriage. The children were all entering their teenage years, and each had developed a strong, unique personality. Jerry loved Lisa and believed he could be a good friend and provider for the children. He hoped for harmony in their home and needed to know, before actually proposing to Lisa, if he could establish a friendship with each of the children one by one. He feared that he could not take on the responsibilities of such a large, blended family if the children opposed him from the start.

There were plenty of opportunities to spend time with them, once the kids knew their mother was serious about Jerry. At first, like most teenagers, they were interested in what was in it for them; extra rides to and from school events, dances, etc. They wanted to know if Jerry would bring new rules into the house and if so, could they live with them. Could he make his new rules worthwhile to them by offering rewards and incentives for good performance at school and with home chores? Most importantly, could they get along? Was Jerry the type of guy they could live with day to day. Would he try to be their father—they already *had* a father. Would he want them to call him "Dad?"

Jerry and Lisa's engagement lasted as long as it took for them to believe that the whole family could get along. In fact, they believed they would all be better off with each other than they were apart.

Jerry met Lisa's father who said, "It doesn't take long to see what's going on for you two." They were openly in love, openly affectionate, and were already setting up their household as they would have it after marriage. Her father believed strongly in the Mormon religious tradition, to which neither

Jerry or Lisa subscribed. When Jerry asked for his blessing, he said, "To me there is only one right way to get married; in the church. But if you're not going to do that, then more power to you and best of luck."

Jerry was moved by his apparent acceptance of him. Taking a sidelong glance at Lisa he asked, "When did *you* first fall in love with Lisa?" Without hesitating for a moment he named the day she was born, then leaned in and gave her a kiss.

Believing that they'd explored all the options, they set the date and married with confidence, looking forward to their very full but fulfilling life ahead. All went well for a while. Jerry, however, had not considered how the children's biological father would interfere with their new blended family life. Although he was absent, the children carried his memory, his values, and his model of behavior with them wherever they'd go. They had a history that Jerry did not share. And no matter what hardships they'd endured in the past, their biological father was *their father*. The children gave him endless chances to be the good father they wanted him to be, endless chances to forgive him and look to him for something new, something good that would justify their undying affection for him.

If Jerry was not jealous of their devotion to this man, he was saddened that the children did not afford him the same goodwill. If Jerry did something unexpected, like try to set up rules for the kids to share their own telephone and avoid quarreling, then the kids' first reaction was "this is not fair . . . you're not our father . . . how can you do this when I need to have things *my way*." Of course, some resistance from teenagers is to be expected from anyone who exerts authority over them. It was the "you're not our father" part that predisposed them to reject anything new Jerry would offer, even for their own benefit.

The children's loyalty to an authority figure was split between their father and new stepfather. It was hard for them to recognize Jerry's authority without somehow contradicting their father's. It was rare, if ever, that they would think "Hmm, Jerry is doing this new thing. I know he's trying to be helpful and provide for us, but I don't see how this helps. Maybe I better check it out with him or my mom before I tell him how pissed-off I am." Jerry never got the benefit-of-the-doubt.

Unfortunately, Lisa responded to Jerry in the same way as the children. She resisted Jerry's well-intentioned influence in the home and reacted to him as if he *were* the children's father, with whom things didn't end well. Although she had felt close to Jerry throughout their courtship, she was not able to be flexible in her parenting to adjust to Jerry's new influence. She might have been able to take control of the phone issue, deal with the kids directly and leave Jerry out of it. She might have listened to the kids' complaints and then had a chat with Jerry about how they could handle this as a united parental front. But she didn't. This further split the family, and Jerry was excluded.

Before they were married, she and the kids had established a normal routine, a status quo, and a pecking order. Things did not always go smoothly, but they were in control. No matter what Jerry tried to do, he was always an outsider and a usurper of this family dynamic. The absent father, whom Jerry had not even considered in his courtship concerns, was a stronger influence than Jerry himself.

When it looked like they'd reached an impasse, Jerry turned to his parents-in-law for help. But her father literally had no words for him. He wouldn't speak to him. Although they had a friendly relationship when things were going well with the family, he had no comment and certainly no support to offer when things went poorly. He still believed that there was only one right way to marry. Outside of the church, Jerry was on his own. Jerry hadn't understood that his father-in-law's encouragement in the beginning meant that he would give no support in the end.

Jerry had missed a step. He didn't know that he, as stepfather, would always be shadowed by the children's real father. He might not have minded that in general. Jerry did not feel that *he* needed to compete with their father. However, in day-to-day life with the family and through the eyes of the children, he did compete. And he lost.

Going back to the first example, perhaps Sidney Poitier was right to make demands on his new in-laws. He knew for himself what was bearable and what was not. He could stand against the opposition of the world if he had support at home. And he received that support by taking time with his family and in-laws to get to know each other, and really let them get to know him. In that way, they came to accept each other in advance of the wedding and cleared the way for more harmony in their home.

As we discussed before, the disapproval of the in-laws (or previous spouses) can't make-or-break a marriage. But it certainly adds pressure to a marriage, especially when it is already loaded with potential conflicts from blending families, blending cultures, or blending races. Was it always like this?

Historically, when marriages were arranged by the parents, *their* expectations were the *only* things that mattered. Often with the help of a matchmaker, parents would get together to see if the families came from the same backgrounds, cultures, and religions. Families would choose a match who often came from the same neighborhood, church, or synagogue. They discussed a dowry, where the newlyweds would live (separately or in one of the family's homes), and the work the newlyweds were expected to perform. Children from such similar backgrounds implicitly accepted many tasks and role-expectations, and didn't expect them to change dramatically after marriage. (Nowadays, with most of us choosing a mate from disparate backgrounds, we must discover these things for ourselves.) The feelings of the newlyweds did not matter much to the matchmakers. It was believed that they would grow to love each other in a practical, sensible way if not in a romantic way. That would be enough to secure a place for them in their own home and in the extended family.

Sometimes, we hear stories of a son sneaking out to steal a look at his bride-to-be. He already knew where to find her; she would be devoting her time to the family business and maintenance. If he could see her once, see her face and think she was pretty, then he could go forward with the marriage without putting up a fight. We hear stories of daughters talking with other women about their betrothed; was he handsome, was he kind, did he drink, would he beat his wife? So little was left up to them. Not until their wedding night could they dance together, be alone together, begin to get to know each other, and perhaps learn to love each other.

Over time, the custom of arranged marriages was replaced by a courtship where couples could date each other with chaperones. After courting for an appropriate length of time, a suitor would go to the father, as head of the household, and ask for his daughter's hand in marriage. He would ask for *permission*, and he needed it to wed. The will of the parent still held sway over their decisions.

Then that progressed, in our quickly evolving culture, to suitors asking the father for his *approval or blessing*. The couple had taken the authority to decide for themselves, but still paid respect to their elders. They did this for their own good, as we have seen in the previous examples. Authority was beginning to shift from the elder to the younger generation. This seemed reasonable and fair because engaged couples were taking more responsibility for themselves and were more independent of their families of origin.

For the elder generation, this was a loss of authority and a new worry: that the grown children would not choose wisely for themselves. Stripped of their power of old, the elders could judge the new spouse unencumbered by any sense of responsibility for choosing him. Without even knowing him, he was set-up to be resented for being inadequate. "Is this the one we would have chosen for her? Is his family like ours, does he do things the same way? Does he observe our traditions and rituals? Does he value the things that we do?"

Unless he was born into the same "clan" as his betrothed, a pre-wed could hardly help but annoy the elders with his foreign ways. Even if he satisfied their basic expectations, he still might trigger their resentment. He might not fulfill his role properly, in the way they would customarily expect. He might be the best husband and provider for his wife and their grandchildren they could hope for, but his personality was irritating. He might be resented for anything that pointed out to them that he was not a perfect match, not good-enough for their daughter.

Today, most couples in the West would like to have their parents' approval, but ask for it only after *informing them* that they are getting married. In this way, the elders' authority erodes a bit more. When conversation turns to the modern divorce rate, it's not unusual to hear our elders cluck their tongues and remind us of how much better it used to be: divorce was nearly unheard of in the Truman years, in the age of Norman Rockefeller. The problems that cover the front page of the daily newspaper now were never talked about then, if they even existed. No wonder their judgment can be harsh. To them the old ways were better, and the old ways still serve them well in their own marriages.

Can we expect our families to accept our choice to marry?

While pre-weds may wish for their parents' unvarnished approval and support, they most likely will not receive it. Parents, like pre-weds, approve of a match because it's *good-enough*, not because it's perfect. They may tell you "I wish he was more of *this*, or I wish she had more of *that*." But in this world of human imperfections, we accept each other as we are. A father might wish for his daughter to marry a prince, but we see that even the royal houses of Europe have had to come to terms with their blemished humanity.

We decide to love each other, or at least tolerate each other, without expecting to change the other to fit our idea of perfection. Unless there is some glaring concern about one's safety or well-being, a parent is apt to approve *with reservations*.

Perhaps these reservations are so minor, so trivial, you'll never hear about them. Perhaps parents will keep their concerns to themselves because they don't want to meddle or interfere, especially about such small things. Or perhaps they will feel compelled to complain but in a way that does no harm. After all, it is a rare family that doesn't complain about each other a little bit.... Just enough to let off some steam, relieve some frustration. Not enough to alienate a family member or drive him away. "Complaints from the in-laws" may be one of those unsolvable problems that a married couple just needs to manage in the course of a lifetime.

To manage this unsolvable problem, successful marriages and families often turn to humor. We accept that we are now family despite the fact we don't always see eye-to-eye and are not always the best of friends. The greater the problem or discomfort we feel in our family, the greater our need for humor. Therefore, it's no surprise that jokes about the in-laws top the list of popular punch lines.

Have you heard this one?

For sons-in-law: An old man and a young man are traveling on the train. The young man asks: "Excuse me, what time is it?" The old man does not answer. "Excuse me, sir, what time is it?" The old man keeps silent. "Sir, I'm asking you what time is it. Why don't you answer?" The old man says: "Son, the next stop is the last on this route. I don't know you, so you must be a stranger. If I answer you now, I'll have to invite you to my home. You're handsome, and I have a beautiful daughter. You both will fall in love and will want to get married. Tell me, why would I need a son-in-law who can't even afford a watch?"

For mothers-in-law: At a senior citizen's meeting, a couple was celebrating their 50th anniversary. The husband stood up and was telling a story of his dating habits in his youth. It seemed that every time he brought home a girl to meet his mother, his mother didn't like her. So, finally, he started searching until he found a girl who not only looked like his mother and acted like his mother, she even sounded like his mother. So he brought her home one night to have dinner, and his father didn't like her. (The joke doesn't tell us who he married!)

And for in-laws in general: Do you know the difference between outlaws and in-laws? Outlaws are Wanted!

Again, the jokes are important; they really are. We all have to vent our frustrations and get it out of our systems. If the jokes are good-humored and this is just the nature of one's witty repartee with an in-law, then it's not the worst way to get along.

Jokes about daughters-in-law seem to fall into a special category. First, there aren't too many jokes about daughters-in-law. Second, they seem to point out a double standard about how we view that role.

For example: Mrs. Jones was greeted by her friend at a seniors' club. "Oh Mrs. Jones, how are you, how is your daughter?" "My daughter is doing wonderful," replied Mrs. Jones. "She's married to the most wonderful man. He works all day, brings her breakfast and dinner in bed. He pays for a housekeeper and buys her clothes. Honestly, she barely needs to get out of bed all day!"

"Oh, that's wonderful, Mrs. Jones, such a lucky girl. And tell me, how is your son?"

"Oh my son, it's just terrible for him. He's married to this no-good woman; she doesn't cook, she doesn't shop, she doesn't work, she barely gets out of bed all day."

If there is friction between generations, it is most often between the wife and her mother-in-law. Just where one might hope to find some female solidarity between these two, divisions arise. While there are fewer jokes about daughters-in-law, most jokes of this type make fun of the mother-in-law. She is the one who most commonly intervenes in the day-to-day management of the household. She has the most opinions about how things should be run. Perhaps if the friction were between the wife and father-in-law, the traditional husband might step in and be more protective. Humor may protect sons-in-law from most direct verbal assaults, but daughters-in-law have much less protection.

I believe that this stems from our traditional belief that women are homemakers and men are breadwinners. When a man goes out into the world, we expect him to face the slings and arrows of outrageous fortune. We criticize and make jokes about him when he doesn't succeed (but makes his best effort), and laud praise on him when he does. A stable marriage is expected to survive pressures from outside, such as times that are richer and poorer, without falling apart. We even write it into our wedding vows. But when the marriage is threatened from *within* the home, the consequences are potentially more serious. If the marriage falls apart, then who is supposed to pick up the pieces? Who is supposed to care for the sons and daughters of a failed marriage, to help them through their emotional trauma and recovery? If there are children, then who becomes responsible for them? Who is responsible for the expenses? And when that "burden" is shifted to the extended family they ask "who is to blame?" Most often the answer is: the one who was responsible for making the home, the one who proved to be unsuitable for the role. When that happens, a mother-in-law may see the daughter-in-law as "the other woman." She may fall back on the old adage:

"A daughter is a daughter her whole life. But a son is a son 'til he takes a wife."

A traditional mother-in-law gives over the care of her son to the wife, and relies on her to care for him as well as she did. When she judges her daughter-in-law harshly, the conflict may become too serious to joke about.

I believe this is true because the same argument is made against those sons-in-law for whom the traditional roles are reversed: where the wife is the breadwinner and the husband stays home and keeps the house and children. In that case, sons-in-law are equally unprotected when their performance is judged to be lacking. In fact, jokes about stay-at-home husbands and fathers can be very emasculating.

We need this type of humor to protect us from things we really fear. As a threat to a marriage becomes more tangible, more likely to happen, we lose our sense of humor about it. When the jokes aren't funny, the complaints become more overt:

The son-in-law says, "My mother-in-law is the most overbearing woman I've ever met!"

The mother-in-law says, "He is the reason I'm rewriting my will!"

Usually, these are spoken out of earshot of the other person. Again, it's important to be able to vent one's frustration if it helps you cope and carry on. But venting is only helpful for a short time; it doesn't address whatever is causing the pressure to build. Without doing something about the problem, the pressure builds up like a steam engine until you blow again. If the conflict keeps stoking the furnace, keeps getting more frustrating, the cycle may repeat itself. Then the quality of your relationship takes a destructive, downward spiral until the fear is realized and the conflict becomes irreconcilable.

Why is this so important to in-laws? Why do they have such vehement feelings about their children's marriage? In addition to their honest, loving concern, mothers- and fathers-in-law want to believe that their grown children are *self-sufficient*, and their own job (to provide for them) is finished. It is normal for Euro-American parents to expect this of young couples. They draw justification for their belief from biblical principles, especially when the wedding is religious. They quote Genesis 2:24-25, "For this reason a man will leave his father and mother and be united to his wife, and they will become one flesh." That is, a husband is responsible to his spouse first, even before his parents. This implies that they will not need sustained practical support from their parents any longer, and they will make choices based on their own best interest, not the best interest of their parents.

When there are grandchildren, the elders want to believe this even more.

Grandparents often pride themselves on being better grandparents than they were parents. They like to see the grandkids on occasion, spoil them, and then give them back to their parents when they start to whine, or need discipline, or need their diapers changed. When a marriage is in jeopardy, they begin to worry that they will have to change their retirement plans and take more responsibility for their children and grandchildren. Although they may rise to the occasion if needed, they don't relish the idea of giving up their grandparenting role. They may fear that, at their age, they may not be able to do the physical work of parenting. They worry that their precious grandchildren will suffer. Too often, grandparents hear stories from their peers who are raising their grandchildren. How hard it is for them. They hear about it often enough to make it a palpable fear, and they are hard pressed to think it could happen to *them*.

We started this discussion by talking about marrying the in-laws. By now it may be clear that they have a vested interest in your marriage; they hope for the best, and they fear the worst. In the beginning of a marriage, it may be difficult to accept that your in-laws' "intrusions" are meant to be constructive and well-intentioned. As we can see, pre-weds have much to gain by nurturing their relationship with the in-laws, and that in-laws need reassurance for reasons of their own. How do you nurture that relationship? And how can you head off a potential problem before arises? As in Chapter 2, we start by learning what in-laws expect of you as a husband or wife and by clarifying what you expect from them. It takes a conversation. How do you to start a conversation with your partner's parents, and when is the best time to start it?

COURTING YOUR IN-LAWS

Somehow, you two pre-weds found each other, had a few dates, and learned enough about each other that a marriage looked possible. Then one of you may have asked the other, "Why don't you come over and meet my parents?" or "I've told my parents a lot about you, they're really looking forward to meeting you. Why don't you come over?" If you are fortunate enough to have living, caring parents who want to meet, then this is a big step in your relationship. While many people hesitate to take this step (and are sometimes criticized for being afraid of commitment), there is a very respectworthy reason to give pause. It is a milestone in your developing relationship, and it warrants recognition, whether that comes in the form of celebration or nervous avoidance.

As they say in job interviews, you only have one chance to make a first impression. In meeting the in-laws, you are interviewing for the biggest job of your life! Even if you have already decided to marry, even if you only hope for their approval and you're not asking for their permission, you will want to get along well-enough so your relations with the family are a strength and support for you as a couple. As the newcomer, you might wonder:

- Will they give me the third degree?
- Should I try to impress them with everything I've accomplished? Will they think I'm brown-nosing them if I do?
- Should I be open, honest, and try to be their friend?
- What do they know about me already, and will I be welcome?
- What do I want from them?

And finally, who can answer these questions for you? Who else, but your intended spouse.

If you are meeting his/her parents, then you already have a notion of yourself as part of a couple. So, this is a good time to practice *being* a couple. Talk to each other in advance. Take some time together when you won't be interrupted. Try to make yourselves comfortable, so your questions and answers will find comfort. Then, try to keep a few things in mind.

If there could be one goal for you in preparing to meet the parents, let it be this: that *you are united* in the way you see yourselves, on your hopes for the future, and your plans to make your dreams come true. You don't need to have all the answers; no one could possibly expect you would. But it means a lot that you consider these things together and share the same questions, the same uncertainties. Not knowing everything also allows others to express their opinions. It invites others to tell their stories about how they faced similar challenges. It gives you a chance to find out if your in-laws got help when they were starting out, and if it's reasonable to believe they may help you in turn.

Preparing for a conversation in this way is preparing for success. While you may be worried about meeting them, you've already passed one of the greatest pitfalls there is: failing to meet with them at all. You show *respect* for yourself and for them by getting to know them before your marriage. Remember, you are not related *yet*. You still have the right to be responsible to your own best interest. Meeting the family can help you decide if you're ready, if it's wise, to put the marriage's best interest first. No matter the outcome, your meeting demonstrates your respect for yourself, your future spouse and her family.

Listen to them and try to understand their values, what's important to them. It is an act of great respect to go to the parents' home (or to their home turf), make eye contact, and let them see the person their child has grown to love. Watch how they interact; is this the model of marriage that your partner brings to your marriage? Does that feel comfortable to you?

Will you get the third-degree? Maybe not, but it is fair to expect that you will be tested. After all, the role of a husband or wife is a very *trusted* role, and we all learn from childhood to test something before we trust it. It's not an insult to be tested, even if it is difficult. If testing begins to sound like criticism, then you can always put up limits, respectfully. One response might be, "I didn't expect to be talking about this today. I see that it's very important to you. I need to think about it for a while. Let me get back to you." Also, keep in mind what we've already discussed: unsolvable problems can often be managed with humor. If your father-in-law wants a perfect mate for his "princess," he may be disappointed to find out that you're only human. You may find yourself being sympathetic and joking at the same time. *Give it time*; this is only your first meeting.

If things go well, then relations can feel very natural and welcome. If there are some rough spots relating to your in-laws, then talk to your spouse about setting up some boundaries with them. For example, you may respectfully listen to the opinions of others, but in certain areas you are set in your ways. When you agree with your spouse to hold firm to your own beliefs in those areas, then again you present a united front; you show others your solidarity. They may disagree with you, but they can't help but respect you for taking a stand and standing together.

Other problems that commonly come up with the in-laws (and become the brunt of so many jokes) are:

- Annoying habits (ask your spouse, is there a certain etiquette you need to observe?).
- Taboo subjects (are there things you should not discuss, especially at this first meeting? Maybe someone has strong feelings about politics, religion, or sex before marriage. Talk to your spouse about what information about you or the parents is open for discussion, and what needs to remain private).
- Opinions regarding family visits: parents who enjoy having their children come home for the holidays may want to know if you will join them, or if you're going to "take her away" to your own family's home to celebrate. Again, this is something for you, as a couple, to decide. When you're ready, decide for yourselves what schedule is workable for you, and how you might change planned family visits to include other relatives and friends. If your families have conflicting demands, then this may be quite an adjustment for each of you to manage. This is an important topic

because it is often so significance to the families and therefore can stress a new marriage. It is certainly discussed in premarital counseling, and it bears repeating here. Again, listening to the parents may clue you in to what's important in their minds.

Finally, *stay in touch* with the family. "It's very good to meet you. When can we get together again?" Whether things go well or ill at the first meeting, getting together again is so important. You've broken the ice, but it may take a few afternoons or evenings together to start to really relax around each other and feel comfortable. There is much to discuss, many stories to share. If you are planning your wedding with the help of your parents, then you'll be talking a lot about the wedding day. Isn't it equally important to talk about the marriage? The wedding day may be the cover, but what is written in the book?

Brian and Dorothy dated for several years before she introduced him to her parents. Brian was a successful businessman. He was handsome and strong, had a good reputation and had been an officer in the military during his tour. But Brian had been in a previous marriage, and his divorce had not yet been finalized when they decided to get engaged. For all of his good qualities, Dorothy's parents would only say, "He's not available." Eager for grandchildren, they encouraged her to dump him and find someone else. *They* weren't getting any younger, you know!

One day, Dorothy took her parents aside, out of earshot of siblings and passersby, and explained to them for hours that Brian was the man for her, that his divorce would be final soon, and that they intended to marry. Only Dorothy knows all that was said in that room. In the end, she walked out tired but confident. Her mother emerged with a sober expression. She was resigned to accept him, despite this glaring fault. Her father, on the other hand, was not pleased. He said, "It's just not right to date a woman, especially *my daughter*, when you're already married to someone else!"

Dorothy explained the situation to Brian. He knew that she had cleared the way, but there were still serious obstacles ahead. Several months went by, and then he went over to her parents' house by himself. He was dressed nicely and intended to have a civil conversation. But when her father opened the door, his first reaction was to size him up and say, "I think I can take you."

Perhaps he didn't believe they would really come to blows. Or perhaps he wanted to intimidate her father just enough to let him in the door. Her father, who was a strong man but of smaller stature, replied, "Brian, you know you're not the only one who knows how to shoot."

And then he opened the door.

Brian explained that, since Dorothy's last talk with her parents, his divorce had been finalized. Her father listened and nodded his head. Brian started, "I plan to marry your daughter and would like your blessing, but we're getting married with your blessing or without."

Her father listened and took Brian's hand in congratulations. "Brian, when you started dating my beautiful young daughter, even though you were separated you were still a married man. No father wants his daughter to date a married man. Can you tell me that you'd feel differently if our positions were reversed? Now, you tell me you're not married any more, so wonderful. You seem like a good man and my daughter loves you. So when is the wedding?"

Brian was taken aback but shook his hand in earnest. They were married in her parents' backyard by the same clergyman that had married *her* parents so many years before, and they remain happily married these 30 years later. Brian's relationship with her parents is usually cordial, sometimes confrontational, and sometimes funny, just like in the beginning. But Brian has always loved and respected their daughter, his wife, and cared and provided for their beautiful grandchildren. As his father-in-law is fond of saying, "that was all we ever expected from him."

Getting along with your in-laws may be a pleasure from the start, or it might be a lifelong challenge. If so, it may get easier with time and practice. As you get to know each other, become *familiar* with each other, and come to rely on each other, many of the differences that divide families in the beginning don't seem so important after all.

WHAT IF THE PARENTS ARE ABSENT?

When parents are far away, it may take quite a bit more of an effort to contact them. It can still be done by phone, mail, or you may choose to take your next vacation to meet them. Making the effort demonstrates how important it is to you. If your partner is less interested in going, then it still demonstrates respect to her that you are willing to make the effort. And it opens the door to discuss her feelings about her parents with you.

What about parents who have passed on or are not available to meet to offer their approval? If you can't meet them, is it moot to discuss with your partner what they wanted for their children? Can this also be discussed with your partner's surviving relatives? I believe this is definitely not a moot point. Even if our parents (or whoever raised us) are absent, we *each carry within us images of our parents*, their values, and the behaviors they modeled for us as children. Our parents' relationship gave us our first model of what a marriage is like before we could compare it to social norms, scan the news, or ask our neighbors. These stay with us as long as we live and provide some of the basic building blocks of our individual personality. Whether we accept or reject their early model, we come to value relationships by comparing them to our early training.

When a parent is no longer present, then questions you might ask them fall to your partner instead:

- Who was your father/mother to you?
- Did your father call you his Princess? Did he call you something else?
- Did your mother work or stay home?
- Were they openly affectionate, or was open affection frowned on?
- What did they wish for you, and do you wish that for yourself?
- Do you expect me to provide that for you? Do you wish that I could?

Edith was in her mid-20s when she decided to marry Otto. Her parents were no longer with her; they'd been killed in the Holocaust in World War II. Edith herself had been held in one of the concentration camps for 4 years. Although she never talked about it with her family, they knew where she'd been. The experiences she had there determined her sense of self-worth and her ideas about what it meant to be a wife for the rest of her life.

In that horrible situation, she was fortunate to be encamped with her parents before their own death. She had very little, barely enough to survive. Her mother gave Edith her own ration of food even though she was sick and weak herself. "You're a growing girl," she said. "You need it more than me." From her deathbed, her mother taught her how valuable she was to her, and how important it was for her to survive.

Edith's father often told her that he loved her. He called her his Princess and made her believe that her life was precious and worth living, despite the abuse they suffered daily. Edith had one dress, a brown one that she wore every day for 4 years. Fifty years later and after all she'd been through, married, a mother and grandmother, and now safe at home in America with her husband, she still could not wear a brown dress. She remembered the good and the bad her whole life.

When she was rescued and released from the camp, she was orphaned, hungry, and her relatives were far away in a foreign country called the United States. With help, she found her way to them and moved in with her aunt's family. She never complained about nightmares or the horrors she'd seen. Everyone knew that she had nightmares, but it was a different time and the family was eager to move on from the past. Edith brought with her the love and respect she'd been given by her father. She remembered the kindness and quiet resolve of her mother. She grew up knowing that she was a worthwhile person who was capable of love.

When she met Otto, a traditional man who was honest and hardworking, she recognized many of her father's traits in him. He would make a good husband; he would protect her and make her his queen in their home. And she would take the best care of him a traditional wife could, never taking for granted the good life they now enjoyed.

Otto relied on Edith for her strength and her common sense (he had a tendency to be a bit eccentric at times). She was his anchor. She kept him focused on working hard and appreciating what they had. Otto never met her parents, but he lived with their influence every day of his married life. He honored them with the traditional ritual of lighting candles on the anniversaries of their death. It was an important gesture that Edith, again, never took for granted.

So far, we have talked about meeting the in-laws who are included in your lives. Whether they are present or absent, you welcome them or their memory into your home. You find your own place with them on the family tree. For Brian and Dorothy, their in-laws were actively involved in their lives. For Edith and Otto, her parents were included in loving memory. What about those parents who are excluded from your lives? Perhaps they are present, perhaps they are absent. But for some personal reason, you or your partner do not welcome them into your home. Alternately, for some reason the parent does not welcome you into their home. If this is the case, then "courting the in-laws" may be the last thing you want to do. However, barring their physical presence from your home does not necessarily bar their influence from you or your relationship. Their influence, the strong images of them that you carry with you, can enter your life when you least expect it.

There was one young man who was in a hurry to marry before his partner had a chance to meet his parents. He knew that his parents, especially his father, would upset his new wife and treat her horribly. He knew it because his father treated *him* horribly. He wanted to marry early because he feared his partner would back out if she knew what she was getting herself into. It is one of the instances of *male entrapment* that we hear about in counseling. As it turned out and after much heated discussion, they were able to manage their relationship with his father by keeping him at a distance. Later she said, "I would have married you anyway, but I'm not happy you kept secrets from me. Now I have to second-guess everything you tell me. I have to wonder if you're giving me the whole story." They married, but lost some trust in the process that took many years to regain. Their marriage could have gotten off to an easier start if she was a fully informed and consenting partner.

For that couple, the husband was still vulnerable to his father's venal influence. For other couples, an unwelcome parental influence can intrude even if you believe you've done all the thinking and healing you needed to put distance between you. One may feel safe from a bad influence when you're by yourself. However, being married does change things. It can open us up in ways we least expect.

This was the case for Judy and Thomas. In Judy's early life, *something happened*. Exactly what happened was one or more of the types of child abuse we mentioned in Chapter 5. The details don't really matter now. But something definitely happened; it involved her father, and the result was that she would "never speak to him again." Her mother was aware of what had happened, but at the time she was not able to protect her from her father. Now, Judy understands intellectually that her mother was afraid of her father too. That's why she couldn't help her. But Judy could not forgive her mother for failing to protect her when she was being hurt. So she closed the door on her mother, too. As a single woman, Judy was unwavering. Her parents were shut out of her life.

Thomas came from an intact, loving family. His experience as a child was a polar opposite to Judy's. He had no idea how her history of abuse would affect her and their marriage. He had no idea what he should do, if anything, to help her.

Judy and Thomas were living together during their engagement. Although they were both quite young, they were quite independent and self-reliant. They made their own wedding plans. They spoke openly to each other about almost everything. They each felt like they were marrying their best friend. As the wedding day approached and quite unexpectedly, Judy's past began to intrude on their happy plans. She began to have nightmares. She would wake up shouting at her father and lashing out at him. She didn't mean to lash out at Thomas, but Thomas was the one to catch her flailing fists.

Why did her nightmares start now, just as everything was going so well for her? Perhaps because Judy felt safe with Thomas. She believed that he could hold her and also hold this trauma for her. Possibly, they started now because she was passing a milestone in her own life; as she was preparing to become a wife and a mother, she couldn't reconcile the images she carried of her abusive parents with the concept of the parent she wanted to become.

In her dreams, she saw herself cringing in the corner like her mother while Thomas, dressed like her father, lashed out at the child they had not yet conceived. Then she would dream that she was the one lashing out, venting her fury at her own child the way her father used to do to her. Judy would wake up from these dreams hot, sweaty, and disoriented. As she came back to her senses, she realized that Thomas was holding her gently but firmly. He was speaking to her reassuringly. Then she would relax and fall into his arms crying. Although they were alone in the bedroom, they were not alone. Judy's dreams had ushered in her uninvited parents and shattered their prenuptial bliss.

Judy started to get cold feet about the wedding. She was afraid that she wasn't suited to being a mother after all. She thought to herself, "Maybe my whole ugly family story should end with me." She loved Thomas, but feared she couldn't be the wife that he wanted, or the wife that he deserved.

Thomas felt his own dreams of married life slipping away. He didn't know where to turn. He didn't want to ask his parents for advice for fear they might judge Judy and think less of her. He didn't want to share this private thing with his friends even if they could help with such a deeply confusing problem. Instead, he asked the pastor who was planning to marry them. The pastor listened carefully, and then invited them both in for premarital counseling. There, they could speak confidentially and at length about the nightmares and any other concerns they might have without fear of being judged. And they got help from him at a low cost; an important consideration due to their limited budget.

When they started, Judy and Thomas sat in opposite ends of the room. Thomas had this yearning look on his face, and he was worried. Judy sat cross legged, with arms tightly crossed over her sweater. Although she walked in willingly, she looked like she wanted to bolt from the room. It was bad enough, she thought, that she had to suffer her nightmares in private. Now, she had to air her dirty laundry in front of the pastor and spend her waking as well as her sleeping hours dealing with these hateful memories.

Counseling started slowly for them. Over the course of 6 weeks, they became more comfortable talking to this "stranger." The pastor learned all he could about their families and tried to frame their current problems in a way that was clear and useful to them. Then he drew a Family Map for them. On this map, he showed what it was like for Judy when she was growing up. Her family was rigid and authoritarian. Her parents set rules that were inflexible and insensitive to the children's special needs. Further, there was little or no affection in the family. They were disconnected from each other, living separate lives under the same roof. Judy's home was not safe for her. She grew up feeling like there was no place for her to find shelter or comfort. However, there was every chance that she would be harshly punished for the smallest mistakes. No wonder she wanted to get out of the house as quickly as she could and make a home for herself. Now, she found herself afraid that she might bring that old home with her. If that were true, she couldn't bear it.

Thomas' family was quite different. His parents decided things together. They listened to the kids when they had a special need and made adjustments to their routine to accommodate them. Overall, they were pretty flexible in their approach to parenting. They had certain rules of the house that they just would not cross, but they explained their rules so they made sense to the kids, even if they didn't like them. Also, his family was rather affectionate toward each other—good night kisses, regular family dinners where all would talk and laugh about the daily news, and so on. When there was an argument, they would eventually make up and bury the hatchet. No one carried a grudge; in his family, arguments were just a natural part of people living together.

When Judy and Thomas came together, they felt very close and affectionate. In order to maintain their closeness, they each adapted to each other's way of doing things. Judy was more flexible than her parents had been, but she was very rigid compared to Thomas. Thomas, on the other hand, felt that he needed to become even more flexible, more accommodating to Judy when she wanted something done a certain way. He was happy to yield to her most of the time, since Judy was a good organizer and knew how to get things done. And he wanted above all else to protect that intimacy and closeness they had together.

Judy needed to be a good organizer. As a child, it had been chaos in her home. If she wasn't organized, she was lost. Now, she had lost her edge. She wasn't able to organize her dreams. Her first impulse was to just back away from everything; to cringe in the corner, like her mother in her dream, and miss a chance to marry Thomas.

Thomas found the limit to his flexibility. He loved her and was not willing to let her go so easily. With the counselor's help, they both started to understand her dreams and how Judy's childhood would influence their marriage. They talked about what had happened, and agreed that such behavior—child abuse—was never okay and would never be tolerated in their house. They talked about how they would make decisions in the future. Judy needed to hear from Thomas that he would listen to her and give her an equal vote on family matters. They talked about parenting strategies and agreed to take a course together before deciding to get pregnant. Thomas may have had an idea of healthy parenting from his own childhood, but Judy did not. They wanted to be on the same page with each other before bringing another little one into the world.

The work of setting up some structure for their marriage started to reassure Judy. During their final counseling session, she started to relax a little and allowed herself to sit closer to Thomas. They agreed to both act as gatekeepers of Judy's past abuse and make sure it was not transmitted to each other or to their future children. They set that important decision in stone. They also agreed to stay flexible with each other and make joint decisions about family affairs whenever possible. In this way, they reinforced their confidence in their marriage. They regained the closeness and comfort they needed from each other. They knew how to make their home safe.

Last but not least, Judy learned that she could trust Thomas. When she had troubles, he stayed with her, he found help for her, and he included himself in counseling. When times were hard, she trusted him not to leave. She had not intended to test Thomas to see if he were trustworthy, especially not in this way. It turned out, however, that she needed to test him to make sure her past would not repeat itself.

The nightmares did not end all at once. Neither did Thomas' steady presence and comforting. But Judy's cold feet did warm up. With new resolve they married, trusting each other to love fairly and see to each other's needs.

Judy's parents influenced her marriage even though they were excluded. Not only were they excluded, but also their model of married life. Judy said, "It's going to be different than the way my parents raised me. It's going to be better this time." It took some work to replace that earlier model with one of their own. The reward for doing the work was their confidence in the wedding chapel.

HOW A PARENT CAN HELP

From the very first chapter, we've discussed how hard it is, how dangerous it can be, for future parents-in-law to offer advice to a young couple. Unwanted advice can drive a wedge between you, and there's no guarantee that your advice will help. Still, you have a lifetime of wisdom to share, you want to help them get off to a good start, and can't hold your tongue forever. It feels like your damned if you do give advice, and you're damned if you don't. So what's a parent to do?

At this point, many parents throw up there hands and decide just to *be* with their children for better and for worse. Does this mean that you have to be with them in silence?

If you are fortunate enough to have few concerns about their marriage, then it may be easy to remain silent. You can attend their wedding with satisfaction and a sigh. You can reflect on all the good times gone, the wistful memories of growing older, and the achievement of watching your child marry. Songs played at the wedding will celebrate your life well-spent because it has led to this:

> Sunrise, sunset, swiftly flow the years
> One season following another, laden with happiness and tears
> (lyrics by Sheldon Harnick)

If, on the other hand, you do have concerns for the new couple and their marriage, then it may be impossible to remain silent. If so, then how can a parent share their understanding with their grown child? What can they say to help?

Jean Piaget, the brilliant Swiss psychologist, had a different take on the saying "damned if you do, damned if you don't." He began by teaching us about (1) how children of all ages *learn*, and (2) how we can teach them. He saw that children do not learn merely by absorbing lessons and advice from others. He saw that children can memorize and imitate what others teach them, but they need something more to make the lessons their own. They need to be able to put the lessons into their own words, to make sense out of them from their own point of view and according to their own needs. Only then can children *own* what they've been taught and use that teaching to grow, succeed, and feel satisfied.

This is what children do when they play. They take the lessons they've been taught and use them to express themselves in the world as they see it. When children play they become empowered by the lessons they've learned.

They succeed in creating bigger games; they become competent in more advanced ways. In this invented world of play, children digest what they've been taught and incorporate those lessons into their growing and more confident sense of self.

Without play, children feel like they spend their lives merely accommodating to the needs of their elders. They feel stifled when they are constantly forced to obey and adapt to the will of others. They are, in fact, trapped and unable to grow. They may have memorized their lessons and behave appropriately, but they behave only to please their teachers and parents. They do not behave because they see for themselves that the lessons are wise and in their own best interest.

For children to truly learn, they must balance what others teach with what makes sense to them from their own point of view. They must play "without sanction or coercion" from their elders. That is, they must play because it is what they wish to do in order to express themselves. They do not play because an elder approves (sanctions) their play. Nor do they play when they are forced (coerced). Elders can join in children's play only by doing so on the children's terms. Otherwise, the game stops being a means of self-expression and starts to become another lesson in accommodating to others, another lesson in "doing it your way."

Albert Einstein. Courtesy Getty Images.

The founder of the relativity theory Albert Einstein said: "Understanding the atom is the childish game in comparison with the understanding of the childish game."

To return to the original question: How can a parent help children learn? The answer is to give more than lessons and advice. Giving advice is only half the answer. Advice alone will make them feel trapped; it will make them feel like they're being forced to accommodate to the needs of others. The other half of the answer is to help them play and make sense out of what they are taught.

To be with your children when they are expressing themselves, when they are bending the world to suit their own needs and in order to develop their sense of self, is to keep them company while they play. You cannot sanction their play, nor can you force them to change the game. When you do, the game stops and you risk being rejected.

This is exactly what is happening for pre-weds and their parents. Pre-weds are expressing themselves, they are bending the world to suit their own needs, and they are intent on succeeding on their own terms. They need to do this in order to feel independent, competent, and fulfilled. Parents can join in this "game," but they cannot interfere with it. If they do, they risk being rejected.

Parents can join in their children's marriage plans by helping them flesh-out the issues at hand, by helping them consider more fully the gravity of their decisions. They cannot force their grown children to marry or not without risking rejection. And as much as pre-weds want the approval of their parents, they don't want too much of it because that also would be threatening; the marriage might be more for the parents than for themselves.

There are so many things to consider when getting married that, if a parent brings them all up, it might start to sound like you're giving them the third degree. Therefore, for a parent to maintain their balance between being helpful without being interfering, they could likely use some help.

One way to open up their conversation about marriage is to offer the couple this book. You might say something like, "I know you'll make a wonderful couple. There's a lot to think about, and I hope you can talk about your future as much as we talk about the wedding plans. This book might help start a conversation for you."

Another way to help is to direct the couple to some of the resources listed in the chapter on self-counseling. It is a sure bet that tuition for a couple's retreat will never make it onto the wedding registry. However, providing for one of the self-guided counseling programs or even counseling sessions with a professional may be the most valuable gift one could offer. Valuable to you because it helps the couple in realistic ways and removes yourself from the uncomfortable role of offering unwelcome opinions or playing therapist. Valuable to the couple because premarital counseling is a gift of confidence. After looking closely at all a couple's concerns and using all the tools available to a professional, a couple can walk down the aisle with certainty and trust rather than cold feet. It is a gift to the children who may come from the marriage, that their parents cared enough to ask the hard questions and take their best chance on building a happy home.

Through this brief process, pre-weds deepen their knowledge of themselves, their fiancé, and the nature of marriage. They can feel more secure knowing that they are not only "madly in love" but also "of sound mind to marry."

To parents who are struggling with the best way to help their children succeed in marriage, I can speak from my own experience. I encourage you not to hold your tongue but to speak tactfully, sparingly, and to get all the help that you possibly can. Having counseled couples at all stages of premarriage, marriage, and divorce, I have always been impressed by how much good can come from an effective and early intervention, and how much harm can come from missed opportunities. Premarital counseling is the first best opportunity to improve the quality of life of the individuals, the couple, and their children.

Chapter 7

The Possibility of Divorce—Stacking the Odds to Prevent It

Marrying couples believe they have what it takes to beat the odds.

According to modern divorce statistics, about half of the people who get married for the first time will divorce in about 6 years. For second marriages, the divorce rate is 60–70 percent, and the average life of the marriage is even less. For people in stressful jobs and situations, such as law enforcement officers and active-duty military deployed overseas, the divorce rate climbs to 73 percent. Although this last statistic is controversial, the trend is clear.

Despite these staggering statistics, most people believe that divorce will not happen to them. When a group of couples considering marriage was asked, only 11–16 percent acknowledged that divorce was even a remote possibility for them. The 16 percent group consisted of attorneys and law students, a notoriously skeptical population (Potier, *Harvard University Gazette*, October 16, 2003). The romantic in us all wants to believe our marriage will defy the odds.

So why read on? What soon-to-be newlywed wants to be inundated by naysayers and cynics?

Because there's some good news in here too. There are things one can do to improve the odds. As for the pitfalls, it's good to know where there's a threat so you can try to avoid it. To ignore the statistics reminds me of the story of the trail-guide who followed a star but fell in a ditch.

For example, there is increasing evidence that a "good premarital counseling program can help a couple get off to a better start. Further, programs that were offered 6 months or more prior to the wedding date and continuing on for 6 to 12 months after a marriage were most effective. . . . The average participant in a premarital program tends to experience about a 30 percent increase in success. Our findings suggest that premarital prevention programs are generally effective in producing immediate and short-term gains in interpersonal skills and overall relationship quality and that these improvements are significantly better than nonintervention couples in these areas" (Carroll & Doherty 2003, Olson & Knutson 2003). Yet, statistics suggest only 34–40 percent of couples get *any* premarital counseling.

How does counseling make this possible? By bringing up issues and by following-up on developing problems before they become concretized bones of contention. "One of the big problems among couples is they're afraid to ask each other questions. They want the relationship so badly, they don't want to find anything negative that suggests it may not work out," says Mary Ann Bartusis, M.D. Warning signs may be minimized, tough questions never asked.

Reading statistics has other advantages: it educates us about some issues that most people nowadays take for granted. As a case in point, take this news bulletin from March 4, 2005. "Filipino Health Secretary, Manuel Dayrit, announced some very startling news. According to government statistics, as many as 30 percent of Filipinos are unaware that sex can result in babies. 'They do not know how pregnancy happens even though some of them have had numerous children already.' The survey found that in many cases, the couples had not made the connection between having intercourse and having babies and simply believed the children were 'gifts from God'. Dayrit attributed the ignorance over sex to the conservatism of Philippine society. 'A lot of it is cultural because people don't talk about sex,' he said." From our foreign perspective, this seems to be a critical concern for newlyweds, and they should have this information before marriage. But we are all blindsided by our own cultural norms, family norms, and our own wishful thinking. By making ourselves aware of the things we don't know, we take more control of our lives, which might make things a little better for us.

On a lighter note for everyone except the father of the bride, the average cost of a wedding is $21,200 and is expected to rise 6 percent by 2010. Elopement packages are available for considerably less, but the emotional cost of not including family members in the wedding has not been reported. The cost of premarital counseling was not included in these estimates.

In other news, married couples have sex on an average of 61 times per year, or just over once a week. This frequency appears to be age-related. Evidence suggests that those couples who enjoy a healthy, active sex life in their early years continue to have an active sex life in their senior years. This is complicated for some who have medical conditions that require

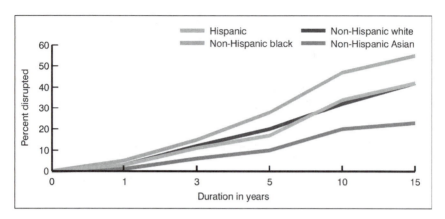

Risk of divorce over the first twenty years of marriage, by ethnicity. Department of Health and Human Services.

medication with sexual side effects. Barring that complication, however, the message is clear: use it or lose it!

And finally, as a measure of how society has changed its views on the breadwinning and childrearing responsibilities of spouses, Aristotle advised "The appropriate age for marriage is around eighteen for girls and thirty-seven for men."

Arlene Dubin, a noted attorney and author of the must-read book *Prenups for Lovers*, observed that although 70 percent of divorces involved financial disputes, most couples don't discuss finances at all until 2 months *after* their marriage. Psychologists, on the other hand, have reported that up to 80 percent of marriages fail because of problems with intimacy. Those problems often develop when the couple communicate poorly or lack the ability to resolve conflicts. After all, who feels like being intimate when you're fighting tooth and claw?

It is very interesting that a lawyer would see so many divorces caused by money, and a psychologist would find so many caused by lack of intimacy and poor communication. Could they both be right? I suspect they are. There are two people involved in any quarrel, and the underlying cause or effect of the quarrel does not have to be the same for each person. Also, it is unlikely that we will report intimacy problems to a lawyer, or ask our psychologist to resolve our money woes. Sometimes, the problem with our marriage depends on who we're talking to.

The communication skills offered in marriage counseling are basically simple language skills and do not require deep soul searching to master. They are presented in brief in Chapter 10. As a psychologist, I believe that assertive communication training is appropriate for a kindergarten curriculum. Yet, I never received formal training in this area until I was studying at the Master's level in graduate school. It is remarkable that the skills that professionals believe can save marriages simply are not being taught. New programs have been designed to address this very issue. Some of them are described in Chapter 9.

So, what are the odds against a marriage? The following chart summarizes marriage successes over time.

The following table summarizes how the marriage survival rate relates to age, race, and education (Raley & Bumpass 2003):

Period estimates of marital dissolution covering 1987 to 1989, using data from the 1990 June CPS

	% Marriages Dissolved				
Duration	5	10	15	20	30
Education					
Not HS Grad	26	39	47	53	60
High School Grad	23	35	43	47	53
Some College	20	32	38	45	51
College Graduate	11	20	25	28	36
Race					
White	19	30	37	42	47
Black	26	44	53	59	70
Age of Marriage					
13–17	37	50	57	63	68
18, 19	30	43	50	55	61
20, 21	22	32	39	44	51
22, 23	15	23	29	33	40
24–26	14	28	34	41	44
27–29	16	28	31	36	39
30+	13	20	23	27	31
Total	20	31	38	43	50

According to the National Center for Health Statistics, 43 percent of first marriages end in divorce within 15 years. That number jumps to about 70 percent for second marriages. Under stressful conditions, such as the long-term deployment facing active-duty military personnel in the Iraqi War, that rate has risen to 73 percent. Divorces among officers tripled from fiscal year 2002 to 2004, according to statistics compiled by the Defense Manpower Data Center. After Operation Iraqi Freedom began, there was an increase of 3,024 divorces Army-wide. Divorce rates run even higher in specific occupations, particularly those that expose people to potentially traumatic events, as well as to heavy responsibilities and public scrutiny. Police officers, for example, face a divorce rates averaging between 66 and 75 percent.

On June 22, 2005, the Agape Press filed this report: A retired U.S. Army officer and military analyst says he is not surprised that the divorce rate among military personnel grew dramatically last year, coinciding with the continued deployments to Iraq and Afghanistan. According to the Army, the most severe trend was among officers, with the divorce rate rising 78 percent since 2003 and reaching more than three and a half times the rate in 2000.

It should be noted that the armed forces are taking proactive and clinically effective steps to combat divorce among the ranks. Clearly, these are remarkable times and their work is not yet done. However, statistics alone are insufficient to bring understanding and compassion for those returning from service from nonveterans. In the interest of supporting our veterans and improving their readjustment back home, I copy here some of the adjustment difficulties veterans are facing. This document was prepared by James Munroe, Ed.D., of the Boston Veterans Healthcare System. Perhaps if we all know better what they're up against, we can provide more support as a whole for the benefit of soldiers and their families.

8 Battlefield Skills That Make Life in the Civilian World Challenging
(Adapted from James Munroe, Ed.D., Boston VA Healthcare System. James.munroe@med.va.gov)

1. **Safety**. Military personnel in the war zone must be on constant alert for danger. Everyday events at home, like a traffic jam, can trigger a sense of danger and vulnerability. The soldier may seek constant control and vigilance. People accustomed to safety may not understand.
2. **Trust and Identifying the Enemy**. To survive, military personnel must learn quickly not to trust in the war zone. It's better to assume that everyone is the enemy until proven otherwise. At home, mistrust and suspiciousness severely damage most important relationships, including marriage.
3. **Mission Orientation**. The primary task in the military is to complete the mission ordered from above. All attention and resources are directed to its completion. In the civilian world, individuals are expected to take initiative, seek out tasks, balance competing priorities, and decide for themselves how to proceed.
4. **Decision Making**. In the war zone, following orders is critical to personal safety, the well-being of comrades, and the success of the mission. Military personnel whose rank requires decision making must give life-and-death orders, even when all the information is not available. At home, especially in families, decision making tends to be cooperative. People take time to consider questions and options and to seek out additional information.

5. **Response Tactics.** In the war zone, survival depends on automatic response to danger. It is critical to act first—with maximum firepower—and think later. Keeping all supplies and equipment, including weapons, clean, well-maintained, and in their proper place is critical to response. At home, messy rooms and dirty dishes feel dangerous, and the soldier's response to these realities may intimidate or frighten family members.

6. **Predictability and Intelligence Control.** In the war zone, troops are in serious danger if the enemy can predict their movements, routine, location or intentions. Military personnel learn to vary their routine and withhold information. But at home, employers expect routines and children need them.

7. **Emotional Control.** Combat exposes military personnel to overwhelming events that elicit fear, loss, and grief. Yet the job requires that they move on quickly, staying alert and vigilant. The range of acceptable emotions may narrow to anger and irritability. Drugs and alcohol help sustain emotional numbing, even after the soldier comes home. Emotions that are dangerous in combat are critical for relationships at home.

8. **Talking about the War.** It's hard to talk about how the war changed the individual. War may challenge the soldier's core beliefs about humanity and justice in the world. There are few opportunities to reflect on this in the combat situation. At home, it is difficult to explain to civilians—to people who live in safety—what happened in combat, what decisions were made, why those decisions were necessary. Talking about the war may overwhelm the soldier with horror or grief. And the soldier may be afraid that their stories will upset people they care about or lead to rejection.

A final word about these maladaptive traits observed in soldiers returning from war. The most common diagnosis for individuals with this constellation of symptoms is PTSD: Posttraumatic Stress Disorder. As we already know, this disorder is not confined to soldiers or to war. Anyone who has endured and survived a life-threatening situation, or even a situation that they believed to be life-threatening such as domestic violence or child/spousal abuse, can assume defensive postures like those described above.

For 3 years, I was the staff psychologist in a county juvenile correctional facility. The most common diagnosis of the kids I saw there was PTSD. With few exceptions, the source of their trauma was domestic violence; more often than not, chronic domestic violence. The effects of exposure to such trauma is long lasting. It can sometimes last lifelong. It is important to know that the spouse of a person suffering with PTSD is limited in her ability to intervene in a therapeutic way by the very nature of the role as spouse. Sometimes help is needed from professionals, from someone outside of the family who is more "objective" about problems that come to the surface. More often, help is needed from peers who have experienced similar trauma. That is, for individuals with PTSD or PTSD-like symptoms, therapy in a group situation may be the treatment of choice.

As we collectively try to limit violence and trauma in our homes and on our streets, we must remember that the ghosts of traumatic events haunt the survivors, their homes, and marriages long after the event has past and the physical wounds have healed. For those who continue to suffer from the trauma, try to take comfort in the compassion of friends and loved ones. But also be proactive in seeking help from outside your family. The memory of the trauma will never go away. But one can arrive at a place where it can be remembered without being relived. Then one is free of the past and free to live as one chooses in the present. Sadder and wiser no doubt, but free.

TWO WAYS TO USE STATISTICS

As a guide—this body of research has given us a map showing many of the high points our dialogue needs to travel.

For every theory and every significant factor described above, ask yourself this: "where do we fit into this? How does this apply to us?" Notice where you feel most compatible, most connected. These are your strengths; support them. Notice when a red flag goes up, when you identify yourself fitting into a high-risk group. When you discover an aspect in your relationship that generates some friction, focus on it. Know it well. Then decide what to do about it. What researchers call a "negative indicator" *should be read by pre-weds* as a focus for concern and discussion. It need not threaten your relationship at all. To recall Gottman, "69% of a couple's problems are *managed* not *solved*."

It can be very reassuring to know your limits with your partner. There will always be differences between two strong people. Our differences can be something to celebrate; they needn't generate friction. And there is already cause for optimism. By reading this book and trying to take these many points personally, you already belong in the highly successful group that started premarital counseling early. That group, you recall, increased their chances of success in marriage by 30 percent.

A couple can go far on this self-guided dialogue of marriage. For the next few chapters we continue to look at different aspects of marriage and take a larger context of this great event. In Chapter 9 and the appendices, couples are given a number of questions and exercises to address. These questions are not *tests* and there are no right or wrong answers. They are simply aids to focus in on which issues are significant to you.

At the end of those exercises, some couples may still be curious about certain things and wish for a deeper conversation. Others may have discovered that they differ in opinion on a number of issues and might benefit from mediation. For those people, formal counseling may be useful. The therapist will have access to instruments that measure personality, compatibility, attitude, etc., which a couple cannot provide for themselves. For those of you who are required by your church to attend premarital counseling, consider using what you're learning here to ask pointed questions of your clergy. Try to make the best use of all your time.

There is an alternative use for statistics, and that is from a historical perspective. In hindsight, we can see what has succeeded and what has not. We are inclined to read statistics with hindsight because that is how research is written. The couples cited in research have become statistics. While there are many encouraging success stories, many of the prospects seem grim and daunting. They do not empower us to approach marriage at all, much less to approach with optimistic caution. One might lament: "These statistics are a sign of a loss of a dream. People don't get married to divorce," said Army Chaplain Col. Glen Bloomstrom.

There is so much to consider, it is no wonder so many couples skip the critical-thinking phase of engagement and go straight to the wedding. However, if research shows us anything, it is this: these issues come up sooner or later unavoidably. At this time when you have the highest mutual regard for yourselves, you have the best chance to come to terms with all concerns.

Up until now, we have referred to *couples considering marriage*. Let's change that to *couples engaged to be married*. Truly, two people cannot be more engaged on a sustained, intimate basis, than here in conversation about the many faces of their marriage.

Chapter 8

Changing Your Mind—Deciding Not to Marry Now

How can you tell the difference between pre-wedding jitters and your better judgment advising you against getting married? One's moral certainty can be confounded when considering the best and the worst-case scenarios with head and heart. So far, we have not avoided difficult topics. Now, let's consider how to sensibly weigh that decision.

This chapter may be the most difficult for some couples to read since it deals with changing your mind and deciding not to marry, at least not now. While canceling a wedding can be a wedding planner's nightmare, it may be the smartest decision for those who have serious doubts.

I strongly believe that it is in a couple's vital interest to face their uncertainties about each other and about marriage before saying "I do." As we've seen, going through the motions of getting married isn't nearly as challenging as getting to know each other on a deeper level before the ceremony. When couples meet that challenge together, their chances of enjoying a satisfying, intimate married life are greatly enhanced. By the same token, when a couple decides not to marry and are honest and forthright with each other about it, their chances of preserving their friendship, and perhaps even a wedding in the future, are greatly enhanced.

Certainly, "being left at the altar" is no way to show respect for yourself or your partner. It is almost certain to arouse sympathy for your partner, and enmity for yourself.

Take, for example, the unhappy fate of John Mason of Atlanta (reported by the *National Review* in May 2005). His bride-to-be went missing shortly before their wedding. Police searches were conducted, a reward was offered, and the worst was feared. It turned out that the bride had cold feet. She showed up in Albuquerque, penniless and distraught, at first claiming to have been kidnapped, but soon confessing that she had fled voluntarily from the looming nuptials. There was some discussion about whether she should be charged with wasting police time.

Perhaps charges should be filed, perhaps not. We can react with some sense of gratitude by knowing that the ceremony of marriage, battered, betrayed, and politicized as it has become, is still taken seriously enough to cause such a reaction in a young woman. Marriage remains a momentous life event—for many of us, as for this Atlanta bride, the most momentous of all.

Of Sound Mind to Marry has been a guide through the process of self-examination and "us-examination." For some, arriving at a greater understanding of your partner, of the person you are becoming as part of a couple, and of the marriage you are about to create has brought to light issues that may appear irreconcilable, at least for *now*. Let's take a look at what some of them may be....

LIVING ON THE EYE OF A DRAGON

According to Chinese tradition, every house is built on some part of the Earth Dragon. To rest on the Dragon's back is ideal. Being on its head or neck is troublesome, as the dragon might lift his head and upset the house built upon it. Being on its eye means it's time to move. It is very hard to consider moving, to consider upsetting your home and getting a divorce. To let the idea nest inside you causes a great sense of loss, even before the last conversation begins.

Some people say that a spouse's love should be unconditional, but I believe that is unrealistic in adult relationships. Some say that unconditional love is reserved for children, from whom we expect unacceptable behavior from time to time as part of their normal and healthy development. In adult relationships, we love conditionally. We extend our love under the condition that we are treated with some level of respect for who we are and with tolerance for our differences, which can be managed when they cannot be resolved.

When arguments and discord arise and resolve is nowhere in sight, the atmosphere within a marriage can become toxic. Spouses are no longer able to respond to each other in the moment, but carry over resentments and harsh judgments from the past. In a vicious circle of disagreements, arguments can become opportunities to rehash ancient wounds, aimed not at mending, but at hurting and letting the other partner know they are hurt. Spouses carry over the stress and fear of their failed encounters to the next one, bringing less hope for resolve to each new "confrontation." They stress themselves and each other.

When communication becomes a *downward spiral*, the best thing to do is to *break the cycle*. Like a child who learns by taking one step backward, two steps forward, a couple can break the cycle of destructive engagement by stepping back or by taking another approach.

The first step in breaking the cycle is to get some help. Whatever that help looks like—a friend's compassionate ear, a couple's retreat, a clergyman, a therapist, a family member, it's time to get it. For those who need suggestions and resources, many are listed in the next chapter. But there is a time limit to how long a person can live in a toxic environment; how much anger and animosity a heart can hold without breaking. There is a critical period in a relationship when getting help can really help heal the wounds a couple is feeling. When a couple consistently reaches an impasse, it is a sure sign that they need help while they're still invested, while they still *want* their relationship enough to engage each other and not withdraw, not accept their impasse as final.

Most readers of this book are still planning their marriage. To emphasize how difficult facing these issues can be *after* marriage, let's look at examples of those who are already married and find themselves in a toxic situation.

I once listened to an expert speak about postpartum depression: a woman's depression that comes after she's birthed her baby. The lecturer described how severely the depression can affect the woman's family and especially her spouse. She may rage against him, blame him, cry out desperately for comfort and support, then coldly reject him when he tries to approach her. His very touch can feel abrasive to her, no matter how gentle. The speaker emphasized how difficult it can be on the husband to remain supportive. She concluded, "A woman with severe depression needs help from family and professionals. But a husband should be aware of his own limits and not stand by and let himself be abused." Unlike child abuse, where others will call for help if abuse is suspected, nobody is going to make that call for you. You are a responsible adult, capable of governing your own behavior. You need to protect yourself.

We tend to talk about help in a hierarchical way. First we get counseling, then therapy, then mediation. We can seek the help we need from a counselor or therapist, clergy, or from the Court mediator. Couples who engaged in premarital counseling may be more open to mediation, since they're more used to a third person working to bridge the gap. Also, a couple who has received counseling in the past may seek help sooner when their goal is still to reconcile, not to separate as amicably as possible.

Hopefully, the mediator can *deescalate* the problems and the angst. If the problems continue, however, then the next step to deescalate a conflict may include a temporary, trial separation. The hope is that, during a trial separation, each spouse will have time to cool off, reflect on their situation, and decide to make amends. Sometimes adults can benefit as much as children from taking a time out. In many States, a trial separation is required before a couple can finally dissolve their marriage.

As an unmarried person, your responsibility is to your own best interest *first*. As a married person, your responsibility is to *the couple* first. Deciding to withdraw from a relationship, even for your own self-preservation, can only be painful. Yet, it is so much less painful before the marriage and the exchange of vows. It is also lends more hope to a budding marriage when one can look out for himself, identify and separate realistic concerns, and still hold the vision of reconciliation.

TRIAL SEPARATION

If you and your partner or spouse choose to separate informally, then you can write your own terms for visiting, counseling, or whatever help is needed. You are still in control.

If you are already married and choose to separate formally, then there is a procedure to observe. The nuptial contract in many states requires that the couple prepare for divorce by considering all of the consequences, including probable spousal and/or child support, visitation rights, custody of children, and division of marital property. For those who have written prenuptial agreements, then most of this has already been negotiated and you are still free to focus on your relationship. Either way, a trial separation sends up a huge red flag that the time to act to save the marriage is *now*. If you have not yet attended counseling or legal mediation, the state may order you to do so. With the Court involved, the vows that are legally enforceable (described in Chapter 3) become the grist for the mill. If one party does not comply with the terms of the separation agreement, a court can enforce the agreement. If at a later date the parties choose to obtain a legal divorce, this contract may be included in the divorce judgment. When this happens, it is very difficult and rare for a couple to remain amicable.

How long should a trial separation last? Again, if you separate informally, then you can decide for yourselves how long you wish to try to reconcile with each other. As a guideline, 33 states have a rule (See I.C. 598.17) that a marriage is "irretrievably broken" when parties have lived apart for one hundred and eighty days, 6 months, except in cases where there is serious marital discord such as abuse, domestic violence, substance abuse, etc,. that prohibit the possibility of reconciliation. In New York State, the period of legal separation before divorce is one year.

In some states, both spouses must agree the marriage is over or the Court can take action to try to preserve the marriage. In most states, however, only one spouse needs to demonstrate an unwillingness to continue relationship. (In separation, the Court can continue the case and order mediation services, etc., but cannot ultimately deny a divorce if one spouse insists upon it.) A couple cannot become happy together just because the state insists upon it.

These many steps are put in the way of divorce because it is such a legally complicated and emotionally trying experience. Ask anyone who has been through a divorce. They would do anything to save a friend from that. One man preparing for his divorce put his feelings like this:

> I loved her. Not being one to trust my feelings, I tested her. Not by setting hurdles before her and waiting for her either to trip or to come sailing over high fences to me. I tested her by being with her, living with her, and seeing how everyday trials brought us closer or drove us apart.
>
> Everyday was different, but our affection stayed the same. Through our moods, we looked forward to the hours at the end of the day when we could be together, best friends and lovers, feeling happy, having fun, and believing beyond hope that we could really have it all together.
>
> Her children, soon to be my step-children, made it even better. We were busy giving them attention and our days were filled with accomplishment. For my efforts, she promised me a lifetime of big family celebrations on the holidays. It was more than I could imagine for myself.
>
> The change came suddenly. It was as if she didn't love me any more. It was as if she never liked me in the first place. She was afraid of me, she didn't trust me. Forget about being intimate with me, she could barely be civil. My presence irritated her. Nothing had changed as far as I could see; there had been no mishap, argument, or injury. I still wanted the honeymoon to last. The vagueness that caused her to change was one of the symptoms. She couldn't tell me what was wrong. To my many queries, she could only tell me what wasn't wrong and let me know how I misunderstood her. But from the time she changed onward, life for us was traumatic. Our time together was marked by rages and tears inconsolable, blame and anger without cause, and lost chances to celebrate. She didn't see the loss, and wouldn't accept help. We were divided in every way.
>
> For me, divorce was unimaginable, unimagined, shameful, and beyond reckoning. The other way out, 'til death do us part,' kept me up nights thinking about it. There were some dark days. I worked like someone in a hurry to live, in a hurry to get through this bad time we'd run into. Life had become unbearable.
>
> To survive, I needed to take back that part of me that I'd given her to love honor and cherish. I needed to take back my heart and my promise from this beautiful woman who wore my ring. When it seemed like the dream we planned to build was all but gone, doused like a smoking campfire, and my best efforts were no help, I told her we were done.
>
> We marry a different person than we divorce. We divorce because a person is already different after we marry. I can't believe that what I loved in her was insincere, or manipulative, or ill intentioned. I can't believe it.

But believing that it was not intentional doesn't make it any better. Then, she was under the influence of Courtship, a single mother saddled with Need, passionately in love with someone New. We married, blended our families, and threaded a camel through the eye of a needle. For a while it was all we had wanted. Too soon, our new roles as husband and wife took on a power of their own. We took on the expectations and dissatisfactions of each other's father, mother, ex-spouse, and loser ex-boyfriends. Our private conversations became crowded with the Ghosts of Relationships Past. (How can they call it Past when nothing has passed?) Our view of each other was veiled; I took on the appearance of someone else who deserved what I got.

Now, our Court date is only a month away. She is angry and hurt, angry and hurt. We need a Judge to decide things for us, since reason is absent in our conversations and property is an instrument of revenge. I don't think Court is the best place to decide if we were right to love. I'm afraid there will be no friendship for us when this is finally over. I haven't even been allowed to say goodbye to the kids. Divorce is more difficult then threading the camel back through the needle. And all the work of loving her is lost.

There are five wedding vows we eagerly take. It seems that they are esteemed differently, perhaps for some intrinsic reason, or perhaps because they are tested at different times. In a difficult marriage, one may suffer incredible hardship because he cannot break the last vow: until death do us part, even if his spouse has already broken the other four (love, honor, cherish, and be faithful). People face tremendous guilt for even considering breaking the final vow. And fairly or not, the one to finally call it quits faces tremendous blame from others for the marriage failing.

About blame: it is useful to be able to *take responsibility* for one's feelings and actions. It can even lead to reconciliation. There does not appear to be anything useful about *blame*. It is a cul-de-sac of hard feelings. If one is truly interested in working things out, then focusing on blame can be indulgent and counterproductive. Feeling blame or blamed can be an honest emotion and need not be suppressed. But it is not a worthy tool to reclaim a marriage, and it can distract from other tools that are more useful.

DIVORCE

In choosing a partner, one can't see how deeply a partner has been hurt by the past until the relationship deepens. It can't be seen until one reaches a deeper level of intimacy than courtship. If a partner then operates from a place centered on that trauma, then there is nothing that one can do. It is one of the tragedies of the human condition.

—Marshall Bush, Ph.D. (2005)

Young lovers often complain about each other being "commitment phobic," that is, hesitant to commit to marry. It seems natural to hesitate before giving yourself wholeheartedly to a great undertaking, especially marriage. Young lovers complain that the phobia to commit causes one to withdraw from the relationship, emotionally if not physically. This is usually observed in men, although women also hesitate with good cause before marrying as well. Similarly, women withdraw emotionally after childbirth when their focus is, of course, on the newborn. Men complain about the same things after childbirth as women do before marriage: that he is forgotten, neglected, unvalued, etc. Both of these times, before marriage and after childbirth, present normative and understandable reasons to partially withdraw one's attention from the relationship. However, I have seen no greater hesitancy or phobic behavior than the avoidance of committing to divorce.

With the finality of divorce, we look back at the marriage and wonder where we lost the dream. Divorce marks the end of tolerance for whatever problem plagued the relationship.

For many couples, hope remains that the couple's differences might be more tolerable after divorce, in a postmarriage friendship, where the expectations on one another are not so high; where the demands of the role of husband or wife are replaced by the lesser demands of a friendship. For some, the problem with marriage is fitting into the role of a spouse. The role-expectations of a spouse are greater than the expectations of a lover, even though cohabiting couples might disagree.

This last point is certainly one for personal reflection: How do I see myself as a husband or a wife? Is it a role that fits my personality, my dream, or my situation in life. Can I reconcile who I am with the role of husband or wife? Can I do that before even considering who I wish to marry? It is mandatory for anyone considering remarriage to come to terms with this issue.

It is possible to be friends after divorce. Many will testify that people sometimes make better friends than spouses. The hope to remain friends after divorce expresses the wish that, even in divorce, love is not totally lost.

For couples with children, it is necessary to maintain continued interactions with each other in order to facilitate child visitation. These interactions provide opportunities for a new friendship to develop (although the opposite effect can also occur). But there is no denying that divorce represents a great loss. The feelings that ride on the coattails of divorce are intense, and one must be vigilant to avoid being destructive to oneself or to others.

Imagine two hands clasped together. When separation becomes necessary and the hands must release their grip, then resisting separation results only in broken fingers and, in the case of divorce, more severely broken hearts. The trick is to know when to hold on and hope for a better outcome, or when to finally let go.

If there is anything good to be said about divorce, it is this: it is the last means available to end pain that is caused solely by the marriage. After all due consideration, it is the last choice. Should it come to this, then it is in everyone's best interest to make the process of divorce as painless as possible.

As mentioned in the chapter 3, we do ourselves justice by considering all these possibilities in advance, when mutual regard for each other is high. Having decided to separate, then any and all steps that make separation easier are best. I do not believe that making divorce more painful or more punishing improves one's chances of learning from the experience. It benefits no one. Those who try to get even never get ahead. Dragging out the legal process or punishing breaches of moral vows by inflicting casualties through legally enforceable means (usually financial) do not bring satisfaction or retribution or even a reckoning. Nor do they deter divorce.

We marry according to our highest moral principles. If divorce becomes inevitable, then the dignity and memory of love are best served by holding on to those high moral standards, by continuing to put the best interest of oneself, one's partner, family, and children first. No one is a pawn. Everyone deserves some measure of respect. Remember who it was that vowed to marry. Take responsibility for your part in the decision to marry and to divorce. Try to prevent others, especially those closest to you, from being exposed to the poison that ended the marriage.

This is easier said than done. What about hard feelings, real injuries, and lasting damage (from victimization, abandonment, or failure to pay child support?). What if "forgive and forget" is totally out of the question? What if hatred is all that's left in the cinders of affection (Walter Raleigh)?

> I imagine one of the reasons people cling to their hates so stubbornly is because they sense, once hate is gone, they will be forced to deal with pain.
> —James Baldwin

No one forgets divorce. If forgetting also meant that one lost the memory of the joys of marriage, brief as they may seem from this perspective, then no one would want to forget. We are often counseled to forgive. For those who were truly injured by a conflict, forgiveness may be as unthinkable as divorce once was. For most of us, I believe we are counseled to forgive or seek forgiveness too soon, before we've had a chance to have our own feelings and reactions to what happened. To forgive prematurely could be to repress the bitterness of separation and foreclose on the opportunity to see how it has influenced us and what changes are needed to regain health. Forgiveness can be a very distant emotion; a very distant goal.

There is another alternative to forgive and forget. It is to honestly consider the intolerance that caused the separation. Once the separation has occurred and one's safety and immediate security are reestablished, then one's thoughts about marriage could be guided toward tolerance. One does not need to approve of another to understand him. One does not need to approve of another when you no longer rely on him. One does not need to negotiate a truce when the battle has been disengaged. By being able to understand yourself, your ex-spouse, and the history you shared, one may be able to arrive at a point of compassion for each of you.

What was attempted in marriage was courageous, what was lost in divorce is sad, just sad. If one can tolerate that sadness without numbing out, without withdrawing into a shell, without acting out in dramatic ways, then there is room for compassion, even sympathy, and healing. With compassion things become less confusing. There's a chance to get a bird's eye view and move on in one's life. Compassion is permissive. It does not require anyone to change. It accepts things as they are, complete with the emotional loading that comes with it.

Compassion is a double-edged sword: it makes the pain more bearable by accepting it for what it is, and it increases the pain we bear by making us more aware of the pain around us and within us. We married with a great depth of feeling. We also divorce with a great depth of feeling. Few truly wish to feel less deeply, to be less moved by the vicissitudes of life. It is our ability to tolerate these powerful negative emotions that enable us to embrace the positive every chance we get.

RETAKING CONTROL

If you find yourself in divorce, then consider this: Take the high ground. Try to take responsibility for your contribution to the problem. Think about yourself, think for yourself. Consider how you may accomplish, in the precious time left on Earth, how best to live effectively and without regret. If you cannot or have not yet found a way to participate in what can still be the best of times, then make this is a goal. Be open to new opportunities and new ways of looking at things. In the meantime, try to do yourself no harm. To a divorcing person, the future is hard to see. Few people who divorce thought they would ever come to this; it is too much to expect to see far beyond it. Try not to look too far ahead or draw conclusions about love and marriage from this perspective. Trying to do so rarely helps, is often inaccurate, and serves primarily to distract from the emotions inundating you at this moment.

Guard your health. Treat yourself well. Get *all* the help you can muster. Don't be alone too long. You are not alone and others, friends, family or therapist, can help find words for your pain, lend a sympathetic ear, offer outlets for your abundant creative powers, and be your friend. If you notice yourself having symptoms of anxiety or depression, then consider seeing your doctor. Symptoms may appear as: insomnia, nightmares, excessive rumination, substance abuse, sexual acting out, tension in your body, in your shoulders, in your jaw, or gastrointestinal system. Your doctor may be able to prescribe something to help you through this *brief* period of difficult adjustment.

Although it may be difficult, especially now in this worst case scenario, try to be a friend to yourself. After all, you are with yourself for as long as you live. Wouldn't it be best if you treated yourself like a friend?

Chapter 9

Smart Move: Premarital Counseling and Self-Counseling

> I don't know half of you half as well as I should like, and I like less than half of you half as well as you deserve . . .
>
> —Bilbo Baggins

There is much a couple can do to prepare for marriage on their own. You've already read this book and had a chance to do a couple of quizzes. Although you may decide later to involve a counselor in your conversation, now is the time for some *plain talk* about some very private matters

JUST BETWEEN YOU AND ME

The engaged are already in conversation. In counseling yourselves, what is the best way to guide and direct the conversation?

The majority of experts place value on various questionnaires or assessment tools to find areas of strength and growth. The instruments that are available to laypersons offer measures of attitudes, beliefs, and values and measures of *normative* personalities. Personality was high on the list of key elements to a successful marriage, and personality was the slowest to make itself known. Therefore, exercises that make one's personality more visible to himself and his fiancée could be most useful.

Except for some psychological instruments only offered by psychologists such as the Minnesota Multiphasic Personality Inventory, Millon Clinical Multiaxial Inventory, or Rorschach, the narrative approach has been the most revealing technique for understanding one's personality. That is, when someone tells their story, the *way* they tell it tells a lot about them. Therefore, telling your stories is a promising place to begin.

Take this first opportunity to write three letters on the following three topics. Write as if you were explaining it to someone who knows nothing about your background. Take your time. Set time aside to focus your full attention without interruption. Do not discuss your thoughts or share your letters with your fiancé (yet).

a. Why do you wish to marry this person?
    This is the easy one. Pay attention to not only the qualities that attract you, but also those qualities that make him/her a good husband/wife.
b. Explain why your past relationship ended (reasons for the separation).
    Try to talk about your feelings about the issues, the way you reacted to things, and your contribution to the problems. If there was no past relationship, then talk about leaving home and how that separation was accomplished. What was challenging or problematic in leaving?
c. Explain your rationale for believing that this won't happen again.
    Again, what is it about you that has changed/grown that enables you to break from the past without fear of repeating past negative behavior? What is your personal responsibility in regard to this issue?

When both partners are finished (in usually a week), exchange them in this way: Set aside two hours where you can be uninterrupted. Exchange *the first letter only*, and decide if you would like your fiancée to read it or if you would like to read it aloud. Finish reading both letters before commenting. Then speak freely about what you have heard. Consider that the qualities your fiancée valued in her letter may indicate what she will expect of you. Ask yourself if this is true and fair to expect. Is this balanced with those things you admire and expect of her?

Notice the time. If you can repeat this process with the second letter without interruption, then begin. In conversation, consider how much emotional closure is being expressed, or if there are still bleeding wounds from the past. Notice your own feelings as you hear your fiancée's story. Are you moved to sympathy, to rescue, to understand, to anger, or something else? How do you feel about the way your fiancée handled the situation; was the response competent, admirable, weak, or heroic? Given a similar situation, would you handle yourself differently? Are you both able to talk about your own contributions to past discord in a personal and growth-oriented way?

With the third letter, notice *locus of control*: if the narrator feels like he was in control of the situation or out of control. Try to determine if this is a pattern in other relationships. Ask about his personal contributions to the problems, or if he is aware of how his own behavior may perpetuate those problematic dynamics. Where there is a history of victimization and symptoms of posttraumatic stress disorder, then those issues will have an affect on the marriage, but may need to be addressed by the individual separately.

With each question, there are opportunities to notice nuances of attitudes and personality. There is also the opportunity to witness your partner express himself in writing. In the future, if conflict were ever to arise between you, it is some comfort to know that you can revert to communication through writing when face-to-face conversations fail.

After discussion, the letters should then be returned to the partners, not to the authors, to keep and read again on their own.

Other talking points for couples to consider:

d. What is essential to your married relationship?

   For example, a partner with a history of abuse from a previous relationship or childhood may say that a nonabusive relationship is essential. As clear as that requirement is, does it, alone, meet requirements for a sustainable marriage? And does it match the priorities of the other partner?

e. Have you ever been surprised by your partner's reaction to something, especially if it was a negative reaction? What surprised you? What might that say about your partner? How did you react to it at the time?

f. There is an old saying, "You date a man/woman, but you marry the family." What is your feeling about interacting with your potential in-laws? Does that match your partner's feelings?

g. How would you feel if one of your parents or in-laws fell ill and needed to be cared for by you? What would you do? Do both partners feel the same way? Is there anything that needs to be done now to prepare for such an eventuality?

h. What behavior does your partner do that makes you feel loved?

i. Does your partner ever annoy you?

j. Are there behaviors (e.g. spousal abuse, alcoholism, etc.) that you will not tolerate in a marriage?

k. Other talking points on parenting:
   • Is the child wanted or only the pregnancy?
   • When will we be ready for a family?
   • What do we want for a family (financial security, etc.) as opposed to what do we need?

l. Essential reading. One point that has been repeated in this discussion is the need for an engaged couple to make an informed decision regarding prenuptial agreements. The best crash-course on prenups and how they benefit you is Arlene Dubin's book *Prenups for Lovers*. I recommend that each person get a copy and read it in private. Then share salient points with each other. I believe that this is not only a necessary step in the couple's premarital preparation, but also signals the extended families that the couple is preparing to enter the family in a responsible and foresighted way.

These questions, and others that occur to you in the course of discussion, can be revealing. If your answers to yourselves and each other seem compatible, then congratulations! You're off to a great start. If answers came up that suggested that there is still something going on that needs to be worked through, then that might be the indicator for you to bring in a counselor. The extra help might really help. And it's a sign of good health to ask for help when you need it.

Being counseled by others is unlike being governed by others, as discussed in Chapter 3. Receiving counseling adds to one's self-control. Couples want to be validated, they want to learn, and they can be open to new tools when the advantages to them are made clear.

Counselors have instruments that can give surprising insight in a short amount of time. Where issues do exist, they may be able to clarify how this will likely affect the marriage, where the growth points are, and how you may be able to cope with confrontations as they arise. If you choose to recruit the help of a counselor, then you may be able to find one who is competent and compatible from a personal or professional recommendation. You may also find a counselor who uses one of the established programs or assessment instruments now available. Lists of experienced counselors are maintained by the publishers of those instruments.

REVIEW OF POPULAR PREMARITAL COUNSELING PROGRAMS

Workshops for pre-weds, newlyweds, and oldlyweds
Workshops on communication skills and programs on DVD or VHS

This review is not complete by any means. It highlights six of the more popular programs currently offered. The reader may notice considerable overlap in the material offered or the format suggested. I believe this indicates a concurrence of experts' opinion of what is needed in terms of exposure to the breadth and depth of marital issues for a normative couple to be of sound mind to wed. These programs are structured to semistructured. Therefore, couples who have personal issues that they would like to discuss without explicit direction may appreciate private counseling.

Premarital Counseling in the U.S. Military

In response to the tremendous need to help young military couples in this stressful time, the U.S. Military has instituted a premarital counseling program called "P.I.C.K. a Partner," for Premarital Interpersonal Choices and Knowledge.

Company logo: "How to avoid marrying a jerk."

It advises the marriage-bound to study a partner's F.A.C.E.S.—family background, attitudes, compatibility, experiences in previous relationships, and skills they'd bring to the union.

It teaches the lovestruck to pace themselves with a R.A.M. chart—the Relationship Attachment Model—which basically says don't let your sexual involvement exceed your level of commitment or level of knowledge about the other person.

The program was created by former minister John Van Epp of Ohio, who has a doctorate in psychology and a private counseling practice. He teaches it to Army chaplains, who in turn teach it to troops. His program is being taught in 45 states, 7 countries, over 250 military bases, and also in thousands of churches, singles organizations, agencies, and many educational settings. "First, the PICK Program is a five-session curriculum that I developed and have been presenting for the past 10 years . . . The PICK Program is best known by the sassy title, *How to Avoid Marrying a Jerk(ette)*. A video recording of my live, 4 1/2 hour presentation is available in the PICK Products," he states on his Web site.

The program teaches troops not to cave in to the pressure of a ticking clock—like rushing to marry before shipping out for a deployment, or too soon after homecoming. For more information see www.nojerks.com.

The PREPARE/ENRICH Program

The PREPARE/ENRICH program is the most widely used instrument with over 2 million documented administrations. There are two new tools that are especially useful for couples interested in self-counseling. First is the "online direct to couple assessments" available at www.couplecheckup.com. "This online relationship questionnaire guides you and your partner through a series of 110–130 thought provoking questions customized to fit your relationship type and stage. Your answers, regarding a variety of topics, are then immediately processed to produce a 20-page *Couple Checkup Report* with feedback about your specific relationship strengths and growth areas. Alongside this extensive report, you'll receive a detailed *Couple Discussion Guide* full of exercises and ideas to help improve your relationship health."

Company logo: PREPARE/ENRICH [www.prepare-enrich.com; www.couple checkup.com]

There are separate versions for couples who are seriously dating, engaged, or already married couples. If you complete the questionnaires and the results are generally positive, then you can get much of the feedback online and privately that you would otherwise receive only in a counselor's office. If the results suggest that there are many conflicts in your relationship and the feedback requires more thorough explanation, then you would be referred to a counselor via their "Find a Counselor" link.

Second, the new "PREPARE to Last" program is available as a self-directed Wedding Gift Kit. It is a very comprehensive self-counseling program with workbooks, DVDs, Audio Date Night CDs, and the online Couple Checkup. See www.preparetolast.com.

These new offerings are based on the original PREPARE program of four to six sessions that include psychological testing, feedback sessions, reading and homework assignments, and live practice in conflict resolution techniques. It raises issues in a friendly and mild way for the couples to consider. There are separate questionnaires for different populations: those marrying with children, those cohabiting, those marrying at a mature age, etc. To quote Buros, a widely respected test review company, "This measure was developed within the framework of a strong body of research and prior measure development. The current version has been built on the basis of this research....The comprehensiveness of this instrument and the inclusion of an additional set of exercises connected to it should enable this measure to develop as one of the most widely useful assessments in this area" (Fitzpatrick 1995).

"If you want to know how the couple feels about their communication, their finances, their conflict resolution, spiritual beliefs, children & parenting, family & friends, etc., you can get that from PREPARE/ENRICH. The other powerful aspect of our instrument is the inclusion of the couple and family maps, which plot how each person experiences their current relationship and their family of origin on closeness and flexibility. This is the Circumplex Model of Marriage and Family relationships translated into more user-friendly language for couples. It is a powerful way to discuss family of origin differences and screen for extreme relationships that are rigid, enmeshed, disengaged, or chaotic" (Peter J. Larson, Ph.D. LP, Director of Programs & Outreach, Life Innovations, Inc.).

A Brief quiz for couples is offered on their Web site: http://www.prepare-enrich.com/couples.cfm?id=34

From the standpoint of early intervention, perhaps the most attractive part of the PREPARE program is a group program for youth in school or in a church group. The program includes discussion of marriage, dating, family life, relationship skills, and common relationship issues. Each chapter begins with a self-scoring quiz designed with personal and class exercises. Dr. Olson, author of PREPARE, said, "We need to be more proactive and help prevent relationship problems. We need to add the *fourth R* for relationships to the three R's taught in schools. Relationship skills are something that people use everyday. Yet most people have never had a course on how to develop and maintain healthy relationships." PREPARE noted that the *couples' satisfaction with the counseling was directly related to the number of feedback sessions*, which can go as high as six sessions.

Imago Relationships International

Imago Relationships International offers relationship counseling and workshops to learn new skills in communicating with others. Separate workshops are offered for singles, couples, gays and lesbians, and those couples that are deaf or hard of hearing. Imago focuses on building trust in relationships by teaching communication skills which very quickly create a feeling of safety. Many couples immediately experience an opportunity to connect more deeply with their partners, appreciate them more, and revive passion and hope in their relationship.

The workshop includes lectures, written exercises, guided imagery, and live demonstrations of necessary communication skills and processes. Although participants come together in a large group to hear these presentations, you share only with your partner, as confidentiality and safety is maintained throughout the workshop. A staff of support therapists is available to assist you.

You can learn more about building relationship skills by visiting their Web site at http://gettingtheloveyouwant.com. Alternately you can call Imago at (212) 240-7433.

Religious Traditions

Clergy perform most premarital counseling. Many churches require some level of counseling before being married in that church. These sessions are usually offered at low or no fee.

Episcopalian

Mark E. Stanger, Canon Precentor and Associate Pastor at Grace Cathedral, San Francisco, said, "We use the PREPARE/ENRICH program and normally meet with the couple about four times." He also ascribed to William J. Hiebert's construct of premarital counseling.

Catholic

The church uses its own system of Pre-Cana counseling which may vary from church to church. Father Keith Canterbury in Weaverville, CA, reported that they use either 3–5 sessions using a format called "Together for Life," or a weekend workshop called "Engaged Encounter" held in a location nearby the parish. Loyola's program has been described above.

Judaism

Most planning is done one-on-one with the rabbi at the synagogue you've selected, who will advise the couple on the ceremony and any necessary steps. Some synagogues ask them to complete a premarital inventory or other questionnaire, but there's no standard. Depending on their background, they may be encouraged to get tested for certain genetic diseases that occur more frequently in individuals of Ashkenazi Jewish ancestry.

Islam

Muslim couples must agree on a dowry, usually in the form of money, which the groom gives to the bride. They must select at least two witnesses as required for a Muslim wedding. They may be required to meet only once with the Imam for a brief discussion on the wedding, or they may be encouraged to participate in a premarriage course.

Mormon

To be married in the temple, which Mormons believe is holy ground, you need to be "worthy." In premarital sessions, a local Mormon leader sits down with couples and makes sure they are living by the standards of the church. They are tested on such things as their faith, their relationships with their family, their sexual conduct and their use of drugs, alcohol, and tobacco. If they fall short, they can repent, change the behavior, and still be married in the temple.

The Parent Effectiveness Training (P.E.T.)

This course, introduced in 1962, is widely recognized as the first communication skill-based training program for parents. It spawned the widespread parent training movement in the United States and it has been taught to over a million parents in 43 countries around the world. In 1997, Dr. Gordon developed a video-based version of P.E.T. called Family Effectiveness Training (F.E.T.), which has recently been revised and updated. For information on how to enroll, go to gordontraining.com or call 800628-1197.

Free Resources for Parents are available at http://www.gordontraining.com/familyresources.html

The Gottman Institute

Thousands of couples have attended the Gottmans' highly acclaimed workshop, *The Art & Science of Love*, offered four times each year in Seattle. Now, in the privacy of your home and at your own pace, you can experience a personal workshop with Drs. John and Julie Gottman on DVD or videotape, available at www.gottman.com.

DECIDING TO GET HELP

As you can see, there is a lot to consider and organize in counseling sessions. For 60 to 66 percent of nearly wed couples, self-counseling suits their needs, and they do not feel the need for a professional counselor's help. They can get what they need from guides like this one, or from the many resources listed above. If you do choose to consult a counselor, then the task of structuring your conversation will be done for you. You would be free to focus on the content of your discussion, rather than the method you choose.

Consulting a counselor can be a great relief, especially to those who are busy with other things like work, wedding planning, and spending time enjoying your relationship. It can also create some tension because it is difficult to open up to a stranger and share the intimate details of your life, even if he/she is a professional.

For those 1–3 percent of pre-weds who have chosen to have a *covenant marriage*, engaging in professional premarital counseling is a foregone conclusion. Hopefully, *Of Sound Mind to Marry* has been helpful in clarifying the issues you will bring to the consulting room as well as knowing what to look for when you choose a counselor.

For those who are unfamiliar with covenant marriages, here is a brief background. Couples in a covenant marriage agree to obtain premarital counseling before marrying, and accept more limited grounds for divorce. A primary purpose of covenant marriage is to provide both spouses the security and motivation to work hard to make theirs a good marriage by knowing that the other is committed to the same purpose. In Arkansas, Arizona, and Louisiana, the only states where this is available to couples, it is considered a cultural and political response to the no-fault divorce.

Opponents of covenant marriages argue that they are too religious in nature, effectively legalizing a religious view of marriage. Some worry that women (or men) can become trapped in unhealthy marriages—it can be difficult to prove allegations sufficiently for a judge to grant a divorce. However, it is currently still possible to file for divorce in a state that does not recognize covenant marriages (Chapman 2003).

In the next chapter, we'll follow two couples' experience in the consulting room and get an insider's point of view on the process.

Chapter 10

In the Consulting Room

Counseling pre-weds is one of the most rewarding things I do. In my clinical psychology practice, pre-weds are different than any other group of people I see. They come in to the consulting room feeling positive about themselves and their relationship. They do not ask me if getting married is the right thing to do. They've already decided to get married and they are not looking for approval or an endorsement. They come in because they don't want to be blindsided by problems after they've already committed themselves to each other. They come in because they want to make sure they've covered all the bases.

Some couples come in for counseling because, at some point in their private conversation, they reached an impasse and they need help getting past it. Over the course of six counseling sessions, we are able to discuss their concerns in detail. When we succeed in breaking through the impasse, they tell me they are grateful for the time we've shared; that the help they received really helped. They leave with renewed enthusiasm for their marriage and with a sense of achievement; after all the hard work of counseling, they emerge feeling committed to each other and resolved within themselves to marry. They are more confident than ever and very soundly in love. They feel like nothing is standing in their way now.

If a couple finishes premarital counseling and decides to postpone their wedding because some issues remain unresolved, they still leave feeling relieved, like a weight has been lifted off their shoulders. Even if they're disappointed that their wish to marry won't be realized right away, they've had a chance to get to know each other better and become better friends, if not better spouses.

One couple who recently came in for counseling had just this reaction. Although they were living together and had plans to marry, they were already on the verge of breaking up. In fact, he was halfway out the door and ready to leave her one evening, when she became desperate to stop him. She became hysterical and started throwing things. Then, without really intending to do herself harm, she picked up a kitchen knife and slightly grazed her wrist. A few drops of blood were enough to stop him in his tracks.

He closed the door, walked back to her, put one arm around her and with his free hand took away the knife. She had been counting on this. Where before they'd been crying and arguing, now they were quiet and comforting; it was a very strange kind of intimacy.

After bandaging her wrist and talking, talking, talking, he agreed to stay with her under the condition that they get some counseling. She was willing to agree to anything to keep him from leaving. They had to wait 2 weeks for an appointment, but it was the most congenial 2 weeks they'd enjoyed in as many years. There was no fighting, no quarreling. They were both postponing their differences until they could get some help.

In counseling, I was able to help them see that this extreme difficulty, this violent acting-out, stemmed from one individual's issues. Although the violence was certainly exacerbated by her partner's behavior, they seemed to have relatively minor problems in their relationship itself. That is, it was not primarily a couple's issue. Cutting herself as a way to manipulate him to stay was a clear sign of her deeper distress. It was the tip of the iceberg, so to speak. Before I offered them any feedback I said, "I can't really work with you if I'm afraid I might say something that causes you pain, and then you do violence to yourself or each other. Will you promise yourselves and make a contract with me that you will do yourselves no harm? If you get upset, you can argue, tell me off, whatever you want. But if you feel like you're getting close to violence you'll stop, take a time-out, call me or go to hospital. Can we agree on that?"

Again, they both agreed. He looked very relieved. She seemed content; perhaps because she was getting the attention she'd wanted in the first place. Over the course of 6 weeks we discovered that, as a couple, they did have more strengths together than weaknesses. They were good friends, good sex partners, and good help to each other in most things. They had few problems but those problems were, at least at the moment, irreconcilable. Much to her credit, she was able to acknowledge that it was her personal issue that threatened their relationship in this dramatic way. He had more difficulty acknowledging that he had been minimizing their problems, that he had been looking through rose-colored glasses, and as a result had actually enabled her behavior to escalate to this dramatic extreme. When I discussed the kind of individual therapy that might be helpful to her, she agreed to take the referral. He was pleased to see that there was help available. He could be friend and fiancé, and delegate the role of therapist to someone else.

They decided to move into separate, neighboring apartments while she started individual therapy. They would stay in touch regularly, if not daily. When they left the consulting room, she felt reassured that she had not lost him. She might even have found a way to help herself and "win him back." He felt like this might only be a temporary setback for their relationship after all. He'd been ready to abandon everything before he knew that help was available. Now, instead of his despair at losing his relationship, he had hope. I was truly moved by their friendship and the "glue" that held them together, even after such trying times. Before parting, he remembered the positive feedback I'd given them and said, "Maybe we'll see you again next year. Maybe we'll be ready by then." "You know where to find me," I answered.

Who knows what the future has in store for them; certainly not I. After all, I'm only a psychologist, not a psychic. However, it would be great to see them again under better circumstances. That's a success story I would love to hear.

Another difference between pre-weds and other people I counsel is how they feel when they see me outside the consulting room. For example, when I work with someone struggling with disturbing emotions, he often feels awkward if he sees me outside. He doesn't quite know how to relate to me socially after having such a unique and confidential relationship privately. He needs our conversation to remain private, and it somehow violates that privacy to see me living outside that special place. With pre-weds it's very different. Regardless of the outcome of counseling, pre-weds are usually glad to greet me at chance social encounters and are not afraid to share their "counseling adventure stories" with others. Several couples have told me they are excited to read about themselves (in disguised forms) in this book. Premarital counseling is a rite of passage that couples are pleased and proud to complete.

Next week, I've been invited to David and Susan's wedding. They will be beaming, I'm sure, because that's how they looked when they left their last counseling session.

They weren't beaming when we first met; they were nervous and scared. David first approached me at a public event to set-up an appointment. "We're getting married in a couple of months," he said shyly. "Everything is fine with us, but I think there are some things that we better talk over." Susan was nervous, too. She started to say something seemingly inoffensive to David. She said it so quietly I didn't even hear it. Then she interrupted herself, looked at me and blushed, "Maybe this is one of the things we should talk about..." They looked at each other, glanced around to see if anyone was listening, then looked back to me. It seemed like they were afraid to broach a subject because of where it might lead or how I might react. "Of course," I answered, letting them off the hook in this public place, and we agreed on a time to meet in the evenings after work.

Later on, I learned that David and Susan had been living together for nearly 2 years. They had set the date for their wedding before even considering marriage counseling. Then they decided to get help because they had trouble starting a conversation about one of their "hot spots" whether they were in public or in private.

David and Susan are both in their 20s. They're fit, attractive, and very affectionate toward each other. They came to their first session holding hands, and they seemed inseparable as they sat on the sofa together. We chatted for a while about their wedding plans and how much they had to do. Trying to put them at ease, I asked them if they had any questions about me or my background before we started.

It takes some time to warm up for a counseling session. No one wants to walk into a counselor's office—a stranger's office—and launch right into a discussion of their problems. David and Susan seemed relieved when I took the lead and gave them the usual intake forms to fill out. I told them what we were going to do, and they signed the "Agreement to Couples Counseling" that is copied in Appendix 5.

After settling in, I asked them to fill out a questionnaire that consists of about 150 questions. It is a simple, straightforward set of questions that yields very useful insight into one's thoughts and feelings, now and when you were growing up. I asked David if he would mind sitting in another chair. That way, it would be easier for them to answer the questions independently and not be quite so distracted by their body contact. Reluctantly, David moved across the room. Now we were sitting in a triangle, and it would be easier for them to look at each other once our conversation really started.

They finished in about half an hour. "It was easy," they said, "but some of questions were asked many times." Yes, that was true, that was a minor annoyance that the author thought was necessary when he wrote the "test." It was worth the inconvenience because, without an instrument like this one (and a number of them are described in Appendix 5), we would need many counseling sessions to collect the same amount of information. The instrument collected it all in way that was not intrusive or offensive.

There is a protocol that I follow in premarital counseling: a set procedure that organizes our conversation for about six 90-minute sessions. But David and Susan had their own ideas and knew what they wanted to talk about. At least, they knew where to start. They just needed some time to get comfortable with me and this new situation. Then they were ready to tell their story.

When that happens, I am only too willing to put my agenda on hold and let them take the lead. Susan began, "I liked David right from the start, and by our third date I knew I wanted to marry him. He's handsome, he's my best friend, and *we talk about everything*. But I have to admit, since we've started living together some things have come up that just weren't a problem for us before."

David looked like he had to concede this unwanted truth. He was so taken with Susan; it pained him for anything to come between them. "It is true," David said slowly. "We're both under a lot of pressure. Susan's working and going to school. I just started a new job and I haven't got the hang of it yet. And now we've got the wedding to plan, which is a much bigger job than I ever imagined. I'm giving it my all because I really want things to work out as soon as possible. We have plans; we want to buy a house, and start a family. So when I come home, I don't always have the energy that I used to when we were dating. Then, every time we got together was special. Then, the rest of the world seemed to dissolve and disappear when I was with her. She was the only thing I could see. Now our time together is still special, but we have so much to do. It's hard just to focus on ourselves like before."

"I am under a lot of pressure right now," Susan continued. "Between work and getting ready for the wedding, I just need some extra help. For example, I'm a clean-freak. I admit it. I need my home to be clean and I work really hard to keep it that way. David just doesn't seem to care that much about it. I've told him so many times to please put your clothes away, or the dishes away or please don't leave your stuff lying around like that. But nothing seems to change. I get so frustrated some times! It may not sound like a big deal, but when I ask for help, David doesn't even try to give it."

David answered, "I know I'm not as clean as she is. When I come home, I put down my keys, kick off my shoes, and find Susan so I can give her a kiss. Then I let down, maybe for the first time all day. After that, I just don't think about picking up my shoes. I know it bothers her. She complains about it and I say I'll remember next time. But when the next time comes, I'm so tired all I can think about is 'I made it through another day.' It's not because I'm not trying to help."

That was the jist of their first complaint. They were both exhausted by trying to meet their lofty goals. Susan's mind was cluttered by so many details; she fought hard to at least have a home that was uncluttered. David was working so hard he literally gave it all at the office. When he made it home, he let down before he could attend to the things that were important to her. These little things that annoy a person can become so big when you move in together. Somehow, this problem had escalated from David's minor carelessness to "he doesn't even *try* to help," especially now in her hour of need.

Although Susan said they talk about everything, it wasn't clear to me that they always listened to each other. David couldn't remember Susan's wishes when he needed to. Susan never acknowledged that David was making his best effort for *their* best interest. If she heard him say it, he didn't know it. And the conversation went round and round, each time getting more frustrating until they both wanted to give up—but wouldn't.

I thought this complaint was a good start. If this was their biggest problem, then there was help, there were skills to learn, and there was a solution. We had enough time together to go over it all. More importantly, this solvable problem let them test the water in our counseling session: it tested me. If I could help them with this, then maybe I could help with other, more serious issues that might come up.

"It sounds like you're both so exhausted by the effort to be together," I began, "that sometimes it drives you apart. But it is the effort to be together, isn't it? Do you feel like you're each working towards a common goal? Or do you feel like one person is out on their own, just minding his own business and not looking out for the other?"

"Oh, yes. We're definitely trying to build something together," they each agreed.

"If that's the case, then maybe there is a way to deal with it. We can work on that. There are some things you can try. Right now, it seems like it's easy to forget why you're working so hard in the first place. You're so busy accomplishing things that you hardly have time or energy to pat each other on the back; to let each other know that you see each other doing his best. Does that sound about right? Can you take some comfort in that? If you can keep problems like these in perspective, then maybe we can find a way to manage them."

David and Susan each nodded in agreement. They looked tired, and they didn't want to fight. Venting their frustrations seemed to drain them even more. We were nearly out of time, and I wanted give them something to think about and take home with them besides their thoughts of a messy house and a strange new job.

"This week, perhaps you can each take a step back and remember why you're working so hard. I'd like you to write three letters and bring them into our next session. Address the letters to each other, but give them to me. Write them by yourself, and don't share them with each other yet. We'll do that together later on.

"For the first one, write about 'Why I want to marry my partner.'" They nodded their understanding. "The first letter is the easy one. Everyone loves to write about how good their partner is. The second one is a little harder. Write the second letter about 'why your last relationship ended.' (I ask them to write this to see what *can* come between them in their marriage. After all, the best predictor of future behavior is past behavior *unless* one has done some personal work to change their way of relating. I wanted to see if annoyances like their housekeeping issue had also been an issue before, and if it was important enough to them to potentially break them up. Also, the second letter may shed some light on other, more serious concerns elsewhere.) Finally, write the third letter on 'why you believe that problem in your last relationship won't happen again.' Can you do that?"

Yes, they agreed that the homework was no problem. The first letter, at least, would be a pleasure. In later sessions, they would take turns reading them out loud. We would talk about those passages that had meaning or aroused concern for them. Finally, they will exchange the letters and keep them: their first wedding present to each other.

Their first complaint was not forgotten, and they seemed confident we'd get back to it in due time. They each shook my hand as they were leaving. With or without the handshake, it seemed like we had made a connection.

That week I had homework of my own. I processed their questionnaires using a computer-scoring technique. The result was a 15-page report on their strengths and areas-for-growth as a couple. Since the interpretations came from an independent source, it was like having a well-informed consultant in the room with me. I studied the results for an hour then started to feel like I knew where our conversation needed to go.

The first thing to strike me about their profile was the sheer amount of personal information with which they'd entrusted me. I felt great respect for their willingness to talk about intimate and sometimes taboo subjects, and for giving me the very special permission to speak honestly and directly to them. By that I mean, in social conversations it's usually most important to be nice. In counseling, however, it's more important to be honest than nice. Sometimes that means saying things that might be hard to hear, but it's the only way for a counselor to be useful. It sets the role of a counselor apart from that of friends and family who have more to lose by offering an honest opinion, especially if they're not invited to do so.

On their second session, they sat together on the couch and handed me their three letters. I put them away to review later. After complimenting them on their quick follow-up, I gave them their second homework assignment: to buy a book on prenuptial agreements and read it before our sessions were completed. David said, "We've already agreed not to get a prenup." Susan nodded. "I understand," I replied. "I respect your choice. The purpose of this assignment is to be fully informed about prenups and flesh-out your conversation on the matter. It is not to persuade you to get one or not."

That seemed acceptable to them, and they agreed to it without further conversation.

Then I brought up the questionnaires and asked if they were ready for some feedback. They were very interested.

"I just want to remind you," I began. "What we'll be looking at is not my evaluation of you, but rather the way you see yourselves and each other. The different areas covered by this report focus on what's going on now in your relationship as well as some of the forces that are underlying and driving the way you relate to each other."

"Overall, your profile suggests that you have much in common with other Traditional Couples. By that I mean, you agree on most things. You have more strengths than weaknesses. You share most of your values and attitudes toward life and relationships. For example, when it comes to how you want to parent your children, how you get along with friends and family, how you feel about accepting traditional roles as husband and wife, and how you practice your spiritual beliefs, you are both in agreement. You have few 'bones of contention,' and we can focus some special attention on those to make them less touchy."

They looked pleased and relieved to hear such encouraging news. They practically beamed at each other while David brought me further into their confidence. "We talked about a lot of these things on our very first date. We stayed up until three in the morning asking each other 'how do you feel about this or that?' We'd both had bad experiences with people we dated before. So when we felt really attracted to each other, we wanted to see how well we got along about things that mattered most."

They enjoyed having someone else confirm what they already knew about themselves. I said, "What an amazing first date! Did either of you think it was odd to get into such a deep discussion with someone you'd just met?

Susan said, "No, not at all. I was glad to hear him say he felt like I did about so many things. It made me want to spend more time with him, as if maybe this relationship could go somewhere. That first night, it was hard for me to say goodbye."

"It sounds like the saying 'opposites attract' didn't work for you. For you, it was more of a 'like-attracts-like.'" They silently agreed and moved closer to each other on the sofa.

"Are you ready to hear more about your profile? Traditional couples often enjoy the longest marriages. Their marriages last, but they're not always the happiest ones. This is because they mean it when they say 'til death do us part.' They're willing to tolerate much more unhappiness than other couples with less traditional values. If there is unhappiness in their marriage, then it often comes up around differences in your personalities, how well you communicate with each other, and how well you can resolve conflicts when they do arise. Last week, you started to tell me about one conflict that's come up already and how difficult it is to find a solution. Have you made any progress on that one?"

They both shook their heads. Neither seemed pleased to be reminded of their quarrel or how it might be more than just an isolated incident.

"So we can see that communication and conflict resolution are already concerns of yours. Also, if you can't address these problems and find a way to manage them, they can be like a thorn in your side for years to come."

During that and the following sessions, we spent a lot of time discussing communication skills; how to talk, how to listen, and what particular traits or quirks provoked an unwanted reaction in each other. They seemed to get a lot out of our time together; learning how to defuse volatile situations.

They said that each session started a much longer and satisfying conversation when they got home.

Here is a list of some of their prime complaints:

- He doesn't listen to me, or he doesn't follow through with what he says.
- When I talk to her, she doesn't respond. Sometimes, I'll wait for 30 minutes in deafening silence waiting for her to say something, but she doesn't. It drives me crazy.
- He talks over me. I know he needs to give long explanations to clients at work, but I don't need long explanations. I'm not stupid. But when I try to say something, he talks right over me. By the time I can get a word in edgewise, I'm so pissed off I don't even want to talk to him any more.
- She blames me. Maybe I'm not the best I could be, but she says things like "*You* don't even try to help."

Most couples have complaints like these. Although the complaints may start off with problems in communication, they can quickly escalate to personal attacks, like one person feeling "stupid" and the other feeling blamed. Therefore, marriage counselors routinely spend much of their time teaching and helping couples practice *assertive communication skills*. That way, many problems can be nipped in the bud. The actual language skills involved are simple and easy to learn. However, practicing them, especially in situations where emotions are running high, is very difficult. Counselors can teach the whole curriculum in 30 minutes and then spend days, weeks, and longer giving couples a chance to practice in different situations. Here are the skills we teach in a nutshell.

ASSERTIVE COMMUNICATION 101

Being assertive is the middle ground between being passive and being aggressive. When you're assertive, you express yourself and you listen to others without passively accepting the other's message or aggressively reacting to what you believe they said.

There are three simple keys to assertive communication that we'll look at one by one:

1. "You messages,"
2. "I messages," and
3. Listening actively.

"You Messages"

It is a strange quirk of the English language that when a person starts a sentence with the word "you" the other person automatically goes on the defensive. For example, take the sentence "*You make me so mad* when you leave your shoes lying around I could just scream!" The person hearing this automatically feels attacked and blamed. It's his fault that she's mad. His body tenses up. He experiences a fight-or-flight reaction just listening to the first half of the sentence; his adrenaline starts flowing and his heart squeezes in his chest. Without even hearing the substance of her complaint, he gets ready to run away, submit and grovel, or go to battle.

What is so offensive about this sentence? Not the shoes, that's for sure. That's something to deal with, but it isn't threatening in itself; it is not a personal attack. The attack comes when she incorrectly gives her partner the power to control her feelings. Is it really his fault that she feels mad? Does he have the power to *make* her feel mad? This point may sound subtle or nit-picking, but the effects are profound; does anyone have the power to *make* you feel anything? Does he have a tool like an "emotional wrench" that he can turn to crank-up her mad or turn-off her glad?

Of course, no one has a way to grab hold of your feelings as if they were concrete and tangible. Clearly, in the above example she is reacting to a situation that he created. He may be responsible for his shoes, but who is responsible for her feelings? Who *owns* this problem?

As individuals, we each own our feelings just as we own our bodies. We are each responsible for our own feelings. Annoying things happen in our lives all the time. Sometimes, we can do something about it and change the situation. Other times, we cannot and we have to tolerate feeling annoyed. But the feelings are *ours*. They are our own reaction to external stimuli. When you own your feelings, then the other person loses the power to make you feel anything. The difference becomes clear in the second lesson in assertive communication.

"I Messages"

What happens if we rephrase the first sentence to say, "*I feel mad when you* leave your shoes lying around." *I feel*, not *you made me feel*. In this sentence, she takes responsibility for her feelings and lets him know what she's reacting to. When she voices her complaint in this way, he does not immediately go on the defensive. She is not accusing him but rather informing him of her feelings about something.

This gives him a choice. He may be surprised if he didn't already know she was mad or that his behavior was obnoxious. He can decide if he wants to do something about it, respond to her feelings, or express his own. The knee-jerk defensive reaction is replaced by a choice to respond in a way he decides is appropriate. Because he no longer feels defensive or blamed, he has the chance to actually listen to her complaint before responding.

If he responded passively he might say, "I'm so sorry I made you feel mad. It's all my fault and I'll never do it again." With this response, he simultaneously accepts the power to govern her feelings, which is kind of grandiose, and makes a huge promise that may be difficult to keep, probably in order to avoid any further argument.

If he responded aggressively he might say, "You're such a clean freak you get mad if there's a hair out of place. Well, I live here too and if I want to leave my shoes lying around you'll just have to deal with it." Needless to say, this counterattack is not likely to resolve anything. It may put her on the defensive, or they may start fighting with the intensity to splinter steel.

His assertive response may sound something like this, "I can see why that would make you mad. I never wanted to hurt you. I was only eager to kick-off the day so I could be alone with you. I'll try to be more careful about this, because I can see how important it is to you. But I have to be honest, I'm overextended at work and some days I might forget. Please don't take it personally."

Sounds like a very natural response, right? Wrong! When people first start practicing this language skill, it sounds very mechanical and foreign. In fact, that is a fair thing to say to someone when they call you on it. You might say, "Yes, it sounds pretty mechanical to me, too. I'm trying something new; a way to speak more thoughtfully. I'd appreciate it if you could bear with me while I figure this out. However, even though it sounds awkward, I really mean what I'm saying, and I never intended to hurt you by . . . "

In the last part of that sentence, he repeats his message like a broken record. Fight or flight is not an option. He simply expresses himself, let's her know that he understands what she has said, and then he stops. No need for long explanations. He only repeats himself in order to be clear, to emphasize what he's saying, or to let the other person know that this is his only response to that issue. Then it's her turn to speak.

Listening Actively

This final language skill requires the listener to check-in with his partner to make sure he really understood what was said. After hearing a statement, he can simply ask something like, "Do I understand you correctly, that . . . ?" Alternatively, he may state, "I understand that you feel this when that happens . . . " This serves two purposes: It gives her a chance to confirm or correct his understanding, and it interrupts his reflex to react without thinking and possibly miss the point of her complaint. After all, the purpose of communicating is to hear, be heard, and maybe learn something in the process, right? Who wants to go off on a tangent about a misunderstanding? In the above example of an aggressive response, he reacted to his perceived attack. He never addressed the situation or acknowledged her feelings. In his assertive response, he acknowledged her feelings, stated his own, addressed the issue, and then stopped. With an assertive response, he stands a better chance at resolving the issue. If the issue remains unresolved, then at least she can say "I don't agree with his take on the situation, but I liked the way he talked to me. I respect him for that, and I won't be afraid to bring things up in the future."

And that's all there is to it. There are many fine points that come up in the course of training, but these are the salient points. Why, then, does it take so long to be able to use these skills when you need them? What gets in the way of communicating in this simple, straightforward way? What stops a person from being assertive?

The answer is very personal and very different for each of us. In general, the answer is: strong emotions. Our feelings very easily get in the way of listening and speaking clearly.

For David and Susan, learning these skills came very easily. For example, when it came to the shoe incident, they were able to get their messages across assertively. They came to the conclusion that they'd try their best, accept that they had different needs when it came to housekeeping and that they were each *doing* their best, and hire a maid as soon as they could afford one. When it came to Susan's long silences in their conversations, she agreed to *tell* David that she needed some time to think about an issue and ask him to give her that time. It was easy for him to wait once he knew that she was considering what he'd said, and he wasn't left hanging as if he were talking to a wall.

Practicing these skills was very difficult for them when they had strong feelings about an issue. This came up for them in counseling when we brought up the ultimate taboo subject for pre-weds, the prenuptial contract.

Before starting counseling, they had already decided against signing a prenup. However, they followed up on their homework to read a book on the subject, and they did consider it again in light of new information. At the start of each session, I would ask them if any thoughts had come up from their reading. They said that they were learning some new things, but there was nothing remarkable to discuss in session. Then, on our fifth session, everything changed.

Susan walked in to the office with a stern look on her face, walked passed the sofa directly to a separate chair, and plopped herself down with her arms crossed tightly across her waist. She said nothing. David walked in after her with a look of dread. He sat on the sofa, tried and failed to make eye contact with Susan, and then spoke to me. "We were talking about prenups before coming here today. We've pretty much finished reading that book, and I started to tell her what I thought would be fair if we did decide to get a prenup. Susan is really mad at me right now. I thought this would be easy, because right now, neither of us really own very much. We'd already agreed that what was mine would stay mine, and what was hers would stay hers. But we're hoping to have kids in the next couple of years, and if we can manage it, Susan wants to quit work and stay home with them. That's what I want, too. But if something did happen and we did split up, well, I know how nasty things can get because of what happened with my last girlfriend. She was so mad at me that she just started taking everything that she could get her hands on, just to spite me. And we weren't even married! So, I was trying to explain to Susan that, worse came to worse, I'd always support her and the kids. No question about it. But I'm starting to buy tools and equipment at work. If we split up, then I need to keep those things. The book says that everything I buy after we're married would be community property. If Susan walked into my office and started taking things, then I couldn't work or make a living. I couldn't support her or the kids. I'd be ruined! It's not that I don't trust her, but like I said; people change when they split up. She doesn't know this, because she hasn't been through it like I have. I was just trying to tell her that I needed to protect my work or I'd be useless. Now she won't even speak to me . . . "

"Maybe I haven't been through it like you have," Susan blurted out with more fire in her voice than I'd ever heard. "But I'm not naïve. I know what happens in divorce. I saw what happened to my parents. When they split up, I was the one they told their stories to. I think I was the only one my father would confide in. I didn't want to hear all the details of what he did wrong and how bad she felt and why it wasn't his fault. I was just a kid! I didn't want to get in the middle of their fight. They even made me choose which one I wanted to live with! Really, I feel sick just remembering it all. There is no way I could fight the way they did." She turned to face David angrily, "I don't care about your money or your stuff. You can keep it! I just can't believe you think I would do such a thing. Really, I don't think you know me at all."

"Sure, that's how you feel now," he started, catching her glance briefly before she turned away and glared at the floor. He turned to look at me instead. Gesturing with his hands, trying hard to be understood he continued, "It's like the book said, we should talk about these things now when we're feeling good and working well together instead of waiting until we're breaking up. I mean, if we did break up. I don't think you'd do that, Susan. But like I said, if we did break up and you, say, came to my office and started taking things, taking 'your half,' I'd just never recover. And I could never take care of you or the kids if that happened. You're a teacher, what could I do? Walk into your class and take your chalk away?"

"How many times do I have to tell you," she snapped back. "I'm not your old girlfriend. You talk like you have everything, and I have nothing. I have my own career, you know. I can take care of myself. I'm doing that now, aren't I? Maybe you'd be the one to take something I care about. Maybe you'd take the kids away, and not even let me see them." Her words caught in her throat. Hot tears rolled down her face. She didn't try to wipe them away. Looking at me, her voice suddenly changed. "That would be the worst." She despaired and sank into her chair.

"I would never do that," said David.

"And I would never break into your office," she shot back.

David started to speak, then gave up. He'd said it all, more than once. This seemed to be a replay of their conversation before coming to our session. They were stuck; Susan couldn't see through her tears, and David didn't know where to turn.

"David, it sounds like you're not worried about your money, only your need to stay in control of your livelihood." I said quietly. "Yes," he answered, holding his head in his hands.

"Susan, do I understand you, it's not the money that troubles you about this, but that David thinks you could ever attack him or be so vindictive?" She looked at me briefly and nodded, dabbing her face with a tissue.

"You both seem so hurt and misunderstood. There seems to be no way out of this when you're fighting for yourself and thinking the worst of each other. And the worst part you can imagine is that your kids would get caught in the middle."

They listened without moving. They seemed to soften a little, as if hearing their mood reflected for them took the fight out of them. "There is one thing, though, that you both seem to agree on. You both seem dedicated to your children, and never want to leave them or hurt them. Is that right?" They each nodded and looked at each other without anger for the first time that night.

"Maybe there's a way to see this through. Instead of thinking about what you each need or what the other might take, what if we talked about this in terms of what would be best for your family?"

Common ground. They each seemed relieved to find something beyond debate, something they would defend together no matter what happened between them.

After a short silence I continued, "If you did write a prenup, maybe it would be a very simple contract. On one page, you could agree to protect the kids' above all else, even from your own quarrels, and keep control of your separate careers so you'd be able to care for them."

They found nothing to disagree with there. Susan trusted David to be a good father. David hadn't wanted to start a fight or accuse her. They started to talk directly to each other. They let the conversation drift onto other matters and leave their fighting behind. They talked about pressures from in-laws and how to satisfy them. How a prenup could assure their families of their safety and their children's. After their long fight about a prenup, it started to sound like it would solve problems for them, not create them.

When our time was up, Susan stood and stepped closer to David. He said, "I'm glad it worked out like this. I was afraid when we first walked in. I knew we'd talk about this tonight, and I was afraid we'd leave still not speaking to each other. It would have been a long drive home."

Their next session was the last one we'd scheduled. They came in smiling, as if their argument had evaporated in the week since I'd seen them. After settling in, I asked if they had anything they needed to talk about tonight.

"Nope," they said together.

"Did you finish your talk about prenups?"

David said, "Yes, we had a long talk when we got home. We got a lot of things settled, so there's nothing left to say about them now."

"Did you decide to write one?"

"Nope," Susan answered. "We decided we didn't need one." And that's all she said.

"I'm a little surprised. Last week, I thought a prenup would make things easier for you; it would make things easier for your in-laws, and settle things between you about your kids and work."

"We're not getting married to make things easier for other people," David said. "We're doing this for ourselves, and we decided that we don't need one."

They looked very pleased. I was surprised myself that they wouldn't take an easy way to relieve pressure on them when they had a chance. I had to respect them for making the choice for themselves. They trusted each other, and that was ultimately all that mattered.

Their final session was upbeat and cheerful. We'd finished the feedback from their profile, finished with prenups, and reviewed their letters. I handed those letters back to each writer, so they could exchange them before they left. David decided to read his out loud again. This is what he wrote:

Dear Susan,

It feels like an arrival to write why I want to marry you. I've been thinking about it a lot, and after taking some quiet time I'm ready to tell you how I know you're the one to be my wife.

When I first saw you, I felt like I recognized you even though we'd never met before. You're beautiful, graceful and have something about you that sets you apart without a word being spoken. From our first date, I was excited to find we have so much in common. I love that we can talk to each other about anything and value each other's point of view.

Susan, you're fun. You're my best friend. I feel alive when you're with me.

We're both strong willed people. I know we'll butt heads sometimes, but I also know we'll always find ways to work it out. You're smart and capable, and I can count on you to stick with me through hard times as they come up.

We have our differences. You need to keep things straight and orderly, and I don't always help. I put all I've got into everything I do, and when I get home I sometimes depend on you more than is fair to make me the center of attention. I believe things will get easier for us. But if they don't I still believe we'll work it out.

When I've watched you teach your kindergarteners from the back of your classroom, I was amazed at how great you are with them and how they love you. I know you'll be a great mother to our children, too.

Susan, I'm glad to be doing this counseling together to help us get over some of our rough spots. I want to make this work for us so we can marry without any reservations and start a life together that lasts as long as we live.

All my love,
David

When they left, they thanked me again and handed me an invitation. "Would it make you feel awkward if I were there?" I asked.

"Not at all," answered Susan. "We want you to be there."

"I'd be glad to come," I said. With that, they finished their counseling and walked out with each other's letters in hand.

Since writing the above passages, their wedding date arrived. The wedding was beautiful; they had it in a garden on what turned out to be the best day of the season. They had considered every detail, meticulously considered every contingency in advance. They looked like they *were* having fun, and their high spirits were contagious. Susan was beautiful, walking carefully across the lawn in high heels. David looked cool and handsome until Susan said her vows. Then he got choked-up and struggled to keep down his tears. That passed, and everyone applauded when they kissed. We couldn't throw rice as we did in the old days, because it harms the birds that eat it later. So we blew bubbles from little bottles they'd placed on our seats before the ceremony began. The wind was filled with rainbow-spheres as they walked arm-in-arm back to the house.

David's brother made a great toast during dinner in which he thanked Susan for making David so happy. "He's much easier to live with since you came into his life," he said, and everyone laughed while David nodded his head and blushed. Later, David threw her garter, Susan threw her bouquet, and all the single people at the party started casting glances about the room, wondering if they'd be next.

Before the dancing started, they made the rounds and thanked their guests for coming. When they came to me, Susan said, "The last few days were so stressful I wanted to call you. I was in a panic because I couldn't find your number." David added, "Yeah, the planning got pretty crazy. I thought, maybe we should have postponed our sessions so we'd have your help at the end."

I looked at them still arm-in-arm, lit like candles even while remembering the hectic times. With the DJ blaring his music and the guests well into their cups, I felt like I was looking into the eye of a hurricane. Caught up in their *joie de vivre* and filled with admiration for all they'd done I said, "But you pulled it off beautifully, and now it's all behind you. There's nothing stopping you now. You can always give me a call next season if you want to check-in. For now, it doesn't look like you need any more help. Thanks for having me."

I don't think they could have smiled any wider; perhaps they kept renewing their smiles with every guest they greeted. When the evening was over, it was hard to remember that this was *their* night. The guests filed out in small parties, still dancing to music in their minds. They'd given us a fine gift we'd always remember. I heard someone say, "Twenty years from now, I'm going to tell their children about this night." Then I understood what the pastor had said during the ceremony about their "love without end" and was very glad to have played a part.

Appendix 1: How Well Do You Know Your Partner?

Dr. John Gottman

One of the most important features of successful couple relationships is the quality of the friendship. Do you know your partner's inner world? Take the quiz below and find out.

(The Love Map quiz and the Bids for Connection quiz were written by Dr. John Gottman and are reprinted from the Web site of The Gottman Institute. Dr. Gottman lives in the United States and is a world-renowned researcher in the area of couples and family relationships. To find out more about workshops and private therapy for couples, training programs for therapists, and relationship products, please visit www.gottman.com.)

1. I can name my partner's best friends.
   ○ yes   ○ no
2. I know what stresses my partner is currently facing.
   ○ yes   ○ no
3. I know the names of some of the people who have been irritating my partner lately.
   ○ yes   ○ no
4. I can tell you some of my partner's life dreams.
   ○ yes   ○ no
5. I can tell you about my partner's basic philosophy of life.
   ○ yes   ○ no
6. I can list the relatives my partner likes the least.
   ○ yes   ○ no

7. I feel that my partner knows me pretty well.
   ○ yes   ○ no
8. When we are apart, I often think fondly of my partner.
   ○ yes   ○ no
9. I often touch or kiss my partner affectionately.
   ○ yes   ○ no
10. My partner really respects me.
    ○ yes   ○ no
11. There is fire and passion in this relationship.
    ○ yes   ○ no
12. Romance is definitely still part of our relationship.
    ○ yes   ○ no
13. My partner appreciates the things I do in this relationship.
    ○ yes   ○ no
14. My partner generally likes my personality.
    ○ yes   ○ no
15. Our sex life is mostly satisfying.
    ○ yes   ○ no
16. At the end of the day my partner is glad to see me.
    ○ yes   ○ no
17. My partner is one of my best friends.
    ○ yes   ○ no
18. We just love talking to each other.
    ○ yes   ○ no
19. There is lots of give and take (both people have influence) in our discussions.
    ○ yes   ○ no
20. My partner listens respectfully, even when we disagree.
    ○ yes   ○ no
21. My partner is usually a great help as a problem solver.
    ○ yes   ○ no
22. We generally mesh well on basic values and goals in life.
    ○ yes   ○ no

Your score: ☐

15 or more yes answers: You have a lot of strength in your relationship. Congratulations!

8 to 14: This is a pivotal time in your relationship. There are many strengths you can build upon but there are also some weaknesses that need your attention.

7 or fewer: Your relationship may be in serious trouble. If this concerns you, you probably still value the relationship enough to try to get help.

Dr. Gottman found that the best predictor of passion and romance in a relationship was . . . you guessed it . . . the quality of the friendship!

Appendix 2: Bids for Connection—The Building Blocks of Emotional Connection

Dr. John Gottman

Bids for connection happen at a very high rate between partners. For example, happy couples "bid" 100 times in 10 minutes. What makes the bids so important? How those bids are made and responded to influences how well that relationship is going to fare over time.

What is a bid for connection? Bids can be verbal or nonverbal. They can be highly physical or come totally from the intellect. They can be sexual or nonsexual. The key is that a bid for connection is an attempt to create connection between two people. Its function is to keep the relationship going forward and in a positive direction.

Bids are the fundamental element of emotional connection. The brief quiz below helps you to assess your style of bidding. Complete each item by indicating how much you agree or disagree with the statement.

(The Love Map quiz and the Bids for Connection quiz were written by Dr. John Gottman and are reprinted from the Web site of The Gottman Institute. Dr. Gottman lives in the United States and is a world-renowned researcher in the area of couples and family relationships. To find out more about workshops and private therapy for couples, training programs for therapists, and relationship products, please visit www.gottman.com.)

1. I sometimes get ignored when I need attention the most.
   ○ strongly disagree
   ○ disagree

○ neutral

○ agree

○ strongly agree

2. This person usually doesn't have a clue as to what I am feeling.

○ strongly disagree

○ disagree

○ neutral

○ agree

○ strongly agree

3. I often have difficulty getting a meaningful conversation going with this person.

○ strongly disagree

○ disagree

○ neutral

○ agree

○ strongly agree

4. I get mad when I don't get the attention I need from this person.

○ strongly disagree

○ disagree

○ neutral

○ agree

○ strongly agree

5. I often find myself becoming irritable with this person.

○ strongly disagree

○ disagree

○ neutral

○ agree

○ strongly agree

6. I often feel irritated that this person isn't on my side.

○ strongly disagree

○ disagree

○ neutral

○ agree

○ strongly agree

7. I have trouble getting this person to listen to me.

○ strongly disagree

○ disagree

○ neutral

○ agree

○ strongly agree

8. I find it difficult to get this person to open up to me.

○ strongly disagree

○ disagree

○ neutral

○ agree
○ strongly agree

9. I have trouble getting this person to talk to me.
   ○ strongly disagree
   ○ disagree
   ○ neutral
   ○ agree
   ○ strongly agree

Scoring:
Strongly disagree: 0
Disagree: 1
Neutral: 2
Agree: 3
Strongly agree: 4

Your score for questions 1–3: ☐
Scores below 8 mean that you are direct in your relationship. This is great news for your relationship, because you have the ability to state clearly what you need from this person. If your score is 8 or higher, you may be too reticent in bidding. The other person in your relationship may feel as if they have to be a mind reader to understand what you need.

Your score for questions 4–6: ☐
Scores below 8 mean that you are not overly forceful in expressing what you need from this person. Your relationship benefits from this quality of yours because it's easier for the other person to hear and understand what you need. If your score is 8 or higher, you may be expressing so much anger in your bidding that you are turning this person away. Maybe this is because of past frustrations, or maybe it is the way your personality is.

Your score for questions 7–9: ☐
If your score is below 8, this means you have a high level of trust in your relationship. If your score is 8 or higher, this reflects a problem with the level of trust in your relationship. You may need to do more to win this person's trust. Some people accomplish this by concentrating more on responding to the other person's bids, rather than trying to get the other person to respond to you.

Appendix 3: Moral Reasoning and Growth Self-Assessment

L. A. Turner and M. E. Pratkanis

Part I To what degree do the following behaviors characterize you?

Stage 1
 I do not use profanity because other people like my parents would disapprove of it and get mad at me.

1	2	3	4	5
Not like me		Somewhat like me		A lot like me

Stage 2
 I will perform my responsibilities only if I get some kind of reward.

1	2	3	4	5
Not like me		Somewhat like me		A lot like me

Stage 3
 I do not eat food in the computer lab because my instructor would not like it.

1	2	3	4	5
Not like me		Somewhat like me		A lot like me

Stage 4
 I do not talk during a fire drill because that is one of the rules.

1	2	3	4	5
Not like me		Somewhat like me		A lot like me

Stage 5
   I pay taxes because it is the law.

1   2   3   4   5
Not like me   Somewhat like me   A lot like me

Stage 6
   I pay taxes not because it is the law, but because it is the right thing to do; if everyone refused to pay their taxes, the social order would break down and everyone would suffer.

1   2   3   4   5
Not like me   Somewhat like me   A lot like me

Part II How would you solve the following scenario:

   A man named Heinz had a dying wife. The wife had an almost fatal disease. The local druggist owned a $20,000 drug that could save her. Heinz could not raise the money in time and he certainly did not have the cash to buy the drug. Heinz therefore made a decision and that night he broke into the drug store and stole some of the medication. Should Heinz have done that?

   These judgments depend not so much on what we can do in a given situation as on what we believe we should do. [Author's note: While it is valuable to think about Heinz from the point of view of an observer, we must remember that our own judgment is tested when we are engaged in the situation and also aroused by it. Therefore, our baseline level of moral reasoning is tested under stress. Stress is less present when we consider the plight of another. Therefore, when answering this question, try to put yourself in Heinz' position rather than an outside observer's.]

Appendix 4: Grounds for Annulment in the Conciliar (Historic Orthodox Christian) Church

Insufficient use of reason (Canon 1095, 10): You or your spouse did not know what was happening during the marriage ceremony because of insanity, mental illness, or a lack of consciousness.

Grave lack of discretionary judgment concerning essential matrimonial rights and duties (Canon 1095, 20): You or your spouse was affected by some serious circumstances or factors that made you unable to judge or evaluate either the decision to marry or the ability to create a true marital relationship.

Psychic-natured incapacity to assume marital obligations (Canon 1095, 30): You or your spouse, at the time of consent, was unable to fulfill the obligations of marriage because of a serious psychological disorder or other condition.

Ignorance about the nature of marriage (Canon 1096, sec. 1): You or your spouse did not know that marriage is a permanent relationship between a man and a woman ordered toward the procreation of offspring by means of some sexual cooperation.

Error of person (Canon 1097, sec. 1): You or your spouse intended to marry a specific individual who was not the individual with whom marriage was celebrated. (For example, mail order brides; otherwise, this rarely occurs in the United States.)

Error about a quality of a person (Canon 1097, sec. 2): You or your spouse intended to marry someone who either possessed or did not possess a certain quality, e.g., social status, marital status, education, religious conviction, freedom from disease, or arrest record. That quality must have been directly and principally intended.

Fraud (Canon 1098): You or your spouse was intentionally deceived about the presence or absence of a quality in the other. The reason for this deception was to obtain consent to marriage.

Total willful exclusion of marriage (Canon 1101, sec. 2): You or your spouse did not intend to contract marriage as the law of the Catholic Church understands marriage. Rather, the ceremony was observed solely as a means of obtaining something other than marriage itself, e.g., to obtain legal status in the country or to legitimize a child.

Willful exclusion of children (Canon 1101, sec. 2): You or your spouse married intending, either explicitly or implicitly, to deny the other's right to sexual acts open to procreation.

Willful exclusion of marital fidelity (Canon 1101, 12): You or your spouse married intending, either explicitly or implicitly, not to remain faithful.

Willful exclusion of marital permanence (Canon 1101, sec. 2): You or your spouse married intending, either explicitly or implicitly, not to create a permanent relationship, retaining an option to divorce.

Future condition (Canon 1102, sec. 2): You or your spouse attached a future condition to your decision to marry, e.g., you will complete your education, your income will be at a certain level, you will remain in this area.

Past condition (Canon 1102, sec. 2): You or your spouse attached a past condition so your decision to marry and that condition did not exist; e.g., I will marry you provided that you have never been married before, I will marry you provided that you have graduated from college.

Present condition (Canon 1102, sec. 2): You or your spouse attached a present condition to your decision to marry and that condition did not exist, e.g., I will marry you provided you don't have any debt.

Force (Canon 1103): You or your spouse married because of an external physical or moral force that you could not resist.

Fear (1103): You or your spouse chose to marry because of fear that was grave and inescapable and was caused by an outside source.

Error regarding marital unity that determined the will (1099): You or your spouse married believing that marriage was not necessarily an exclusive relationship.

Error regarding marital indissolubility that determined the will (Canon 1099): You or your spouse married believing that civil law had the power to dissolve marriage and that remarriage was acceptable after civil divorce.

Error regarding marital sacramental dignity that determined the will (Canon 1099): You and your spouse married believing that marriage is not a religious or sacred relationship but merely a civil contract or arrangement.

Lack of new consent during convalidation (Canons 1157, 1160): After your civil marriage, you and your spouse participated in a Catholic ceremony and you or your spouse believed that (1) you were already married, (2) the Catholic ceremony was merely a blessing, and (3) the consent given during the Catholic ceremony had no real effect.

Appendix 5: Notes to Professionals

In *Premarital and Remarital Counseling*, Robert Stahmann and William Hiebert trace the history of marriage counseling from the earliest days when counseling was solely focused on the individual's contribution to relationship dynamics. Then, counseling evolved to include psychological education as well as education/indoctrination into the religious meaning and obligation of marriage. Now, most counseling focuses on the relational dynamics themselves, with the couple's relationship as the focus of treatment rather than the individual. When conflicted couples are referred for counseling, our approach to that couple may make a historical full-circle, where we need to once again look at the individual's contributions to relationship dynamics.

Therapists primarily see couples who are remarrying, couples where one of the partners is already in treatment, couples referred by clergy when their assessment indicates that they are in the conflicted or devitalized population (20% of the couples screened by PREPARE), and couples who self-refer with significant conflicts they wish to resolve. Additionally, couples may choose a therapist rather than a member of clergy in order to avoid having a dual relationship with the clergy who might already have an established relationship with the couple, family, or community.

Therapists can offer this service as a brief course of counseling or as a psychological evaluation. Organizing sessions as an evaluation has a number of advantages: it sets the scope and purpose of the evaluation, it sets the duration (number of sessions) and a semistructured format so the couple can be informed in advance of what will happen and what is expected, and it clarifies the role of the evaluator. Although a couple or individuals may matriculate into therapy after this evaluation, he is not yet a therapy patient. Therefore, the type of feedback is different; more direct, more directed, and in general offering more of a supportive and descriptive than analytical quality. Couples are not likely to be looking for feedback to discourage their plans for marriage, but to help organize their premarital checklist and develop awareness of issues and skills to cope with them, and identify areas of strength. Experts have noted that it is useful in counseling couples with multiple challenges to emphasize assertive communication and to correct avoidance of issues when they become apparent. None of the protocols in common use include introduction of the idea of prenuptial agreements, although PREPARE noted that financial management is "rarely a strength" for couples.

Common practice indicates that premarital counseling is a brief, four- to six-session evaluation and feedback to help engaged couples direct their energy for growth and the development of a healthy marriage. Client's satisfaction has been correlated to the number of sessions offered. Especially when dealing with conflicted couples or couples with a history of domestic violence, abuse, or previous mental health issues, a six-session evaluation seems appropriate as a starting point. Ninety-minute sessions appear to be standard and allow time for all to participate fully. Sessions could be held weekly in order for the couple to finish homework and reading. Sessions are structured to semistructured and include considerable opportunities for therapeutic intervention. These are in the areas of assertive communication, financial organization, and expectations for the relationship, personality traits, and the quality of couple's interaction. This evaluation is for the confidential use and benefit of the couple only, and makes use of a clinical interview, structured narrative exercises, assigned reading and homework, and psychological testing and feedback.

To avoid the appearance of any bias, the full fee for the evaluation (a flat fee that includes all services rendered) could be paid in full during the first session. Stahmann suggested that the therapist consider offering a "wedding gift" of one follow-up session, six months after the wedding. Whether the therapist offers this *pro bono* or not, a follow-up session is clinically indicated and improves the chances for a positive outcome. At that point, the couple can decide if continued sessions are desired, or if they would like to enroll in a weekend seminar offered by one of the resources listed above (or others).

RECOMMENDED PROTOCOL FOR EVALUATORS

Session I: Introduction, listen to the couple's opening statements about concerns and goals, develop rapport. Next, the following forms and fees could be signed and exchanged:

> Consent for Evaluation Form. A sample consent form is attached below and includes a fee statement.
>
> Release of Information Form is needed if the therapist wishes to converse with other treating professionals in order to receive previous mental health diagnoses or previously administered psychological testing raw data from instruments such as the MCMI or the MMPI. Those data should be carefully examined and used to guide feedback. They do not yield data on the couple's dynamics per se. They may be useful for an individual client who presents with personal issues that are interfering with his/her relationship.
>
> Expected curriculum for the evaluation.

After initial introductions and forms have been signed and exchanged, the therapist could administer the psychological instrument of choice. Common instruments are listed below.

After each partner completes the questionnaire, homework could be assigned to be completed before the next session. Research cited in Chapter 3 indicates that personality and styles of attachment/relating are most closely tied to marital success. It is not appropriate, and few couples would tolerate, administration of psychological instruments such as the MMPI or the MCMI that are designed to detect psychopathology or personality disorganization. The instruments commonly used and recommended illuminate issues of cognitive and behavior dimensions, and raise questions about features and traits in normative personalities. In order to gather impressions of an individual's personality, the narrative approach seems most successful. The therapist can glean significant information about personality and unresolved issues by posing provocative questions to each individual, then allowing them to write their responses in private and at their leisure between sessions. The same questions listed in the above section seem appropriate and useful, although others could be devised. Stahmann and Hiebert have suggested quite a few talking points with interpretative guidelines (Stahmann & Hiebert 1997).

Session II: Collect letters from the clients and save them for private review after the session concludes. In this session, the therapist can begin offering feedback from the testing. Make note of significant interactions between partners and indicators of personality traits. Before the session ends, the therapist could introduce the subject of prenuptial agreements, process initial reactions to the subject, offer brief remarks aimed to destigmatize prenups, and finally give each partner a copy of a primer on prenuptial agreements. As noted above, I recommend Arlene Dubin's book for this purpose (Dubin 2001).

Session III, IV, and V: Continue feedback from testing and from the three letters. Emphasize those issues or concerns that are associated with empirically validated factors of marital success. Take liberty when discussing the letters to explore beliefs, attitudes, and personality traits as they might influence the relationship.

Session VI: This session could be used to summarize findings, point out strengths and areas of growth related to couple interactions. If significant issues remain unresolved, the therapist may wish to suggest that the engagement be extended to allow time to address those issues more thoroughly. The therapist and couple can seek closure of their discussion and make referrals to other professionals as needed, including scheduling a follow-up session for 6 months after the wedding.

Sample Agreement to Couple's Counseling and Evaluation

It is important that you understand in advance that this is an evaluation for your own edification and that an honest and forthright assessment of your individual and couple dynamics are our only concern. There is a possibility that our impressions, conclusions, and recommendations may not be what you desire. It is our wish that strengths can be discussed and their full potential realized, and conflicts can be exposed respectfully in order to facilitate their clearer understanding and how they may be managed constructively.

The evaluation will be conducted by a licensed psychologist who is competent in performing this type of evaluation. Personality inventories and marital satisfaction questionnaires will be administered before any interviews. This allows us to collect a wide range of data and organize the issues while minimizing the cost and time to you. The evaluation also may consist of interviews with each party separately and jointly.

Once the evaluation has begun, we will make every effort to clarify issues and individual responsibilities for those issues. However, some individuals may wish to consult with their own therapist or clergyman privately and in more depth after receiving feedback from this evaluation. We recommend our clients seek therapy if they would find it beneficial. Some people refrain from doing this for fear it will reflect badly on them. We do not feel that this reflects badly on anyone, especially given the stresses of preparation for marriage and, for some, blending families. We encourage you to take care of yourself in this regard and will be happy to provide referrals upon request.

This evaluation is confidential, and discussion of findings is limited to the couple only. If the couple chooses to include other parties in the discussion, then that is their privilege. Additional sessions with the evaluator can be arranged to accommodate consults with other parties.

You will pay a flat fee of (____) before the evaluation is begun. This is the full fee for the evaluation and includes all face-to-face contact, phone calls, test scoring, consultation with lawyers and other professionals involved with the case, as well as report preparation time. The reason the fee is paid up front does not reflect on you but on the reality that this would leave us open to a question as to whether the financial situation had influenced our judgment. This is not an acceptable situation for you or us and we will adhere strictly to this policy in order to avoid it.

If after reviewing this information you have questions, please be sure to discuss them at your initial interview, when we will more fully explain the evaluation procedure you are about to begin.

Client Statement

This information and the procedures of couple's counseling have been explained to me, and I agree to abide by these policies. I have received a copy of this agreement and statement of charges.

DATE _____

SIGNATURE _____

_____

Evaluator Statement

I have reviewed this information with the parties and the parties agree with the policies as evidenced by his/her signature.

DATE _____

SIGNATURE _____

PSYCHOLOGICAL ASSESSMENT

PREPARE/ENRICH

As mentioned before, this is a very useful instrument for discussion of marital dynamics, assertive communication, basic financial concerns, and family of origin issues. If couple has been referred by a member of the clergy, then the couple may already have completed this instrument and the data may be available with an appropriate release of information.

16PF® Couple's Counseling Questionnaire

This well-known instrument serves a dual purpose of eliciting data about marital dynamics with the added plus of describing individual personality traits that may facilitate or encumber couple relations. IPAT's OnSite assessment software or NetAssess® Web-based service can be used to administer, score, and interpret the item responses, producing valuable information in a Couple's Counseling Report. The 16PF Couple's Counseling Questionnaire is a Level CE-2 instrument (see http://www.ipat.com/CE_Track for test user qualification requirements). A sample report is available at: http://www.ipat.com/pdf/ccr.pdf Additional assessment and report information can be found at: http://www.ipat.com/catalog/pdf/CCR.pdf

For in-depth evaluations, different and valuable information can be obtained by generating a 16PF Karson Clinical Report (KCR) from the 16PF Questionnaire. The KCR offers a detailed, clinical perspective of an individual's normal personality profile. This enables a clinician to discriminate between an individual's behavioral patterns that impact a relationship from those issues that arise directly from the couple's joint interactions. A sample KCR is available at: http://www.ipat.com/pdf/kcr.pdf. More information about the KCR can be obtained at http://www.ipat.com/catalog/pdf/KCR.pdf.

Taylor-Johnson Temperament Analysis® (T-JTA®)

This is a valuable standardized assessment instrument and counseling tool. The T-JTA is a personality inventory designed for use in individual, premarital, marital, group, and family counseling. It is currently in extensive use as a diagnostic instrument to determine therapeutic goals and evaluate progress and change, and in direct use with clients as part of the counseling process. It is often used in pastoral counseling.

The T-JTA measures nine personality traits and their bipolar opposites, all of which are important components of and significantly influence personal, scholastic and vocational functioning and interpersonal relationships:

- Nervous/Composed
- Dominant/Submissive
- Expressive-Responsive/Inhibited
- Hostile/Tolerant
- Self-Disciplined/Impulsive

- Depressive/Lighthearted
- Sympathetic/Indifferent
- Subjective/Objective
- Active-Social/Quiet

T-JTA test results pinpoint specific problem areas providing insight into the internal forces that actually produce many of the external complaints or conflicts.

In addition to its application as a personality assessment inventory in working with individuals, the T-JTA is uniquely appropriate for use with couples and family members. The test questions can be answered first as they apply to one's self, and then answered a second time as they apply to another person in T-JTA "Criss-Cross" fashion. This procedure adds a measure of interpersonal perception to the counseling perspective. Similarities, differences or areas of misunderstanding become readily apparent.

A sample set of T-JTA "Criss-Cross" Profiles depict:

- Husband Profile: The husband's self-perception
- Wife Profile: The wife's self-perception
- Couple Profile: A composite of the two self tests
- Husband by Wife: The husband as seen by the wife
- Wife by Husband: The wife as seen by the husband

Trait definitions are included at the bottom of the profile to assist the counselor in describing the meaning of the traits measured. The insights derived from the T-JTA profiled results assist in improving self-understanding and aid the promotion of personal growth and change.

The *Test Manual* is very comprehensive and contains complete coverage of test administration, scoring, and interpretation. Also helpful is the *T-JTA Handbook*—a companion piece to the Test Manual—that provides additional guidelines for interpreting T-JTA results beyond that contained in the manual. The T-JTA Handbook includes a number of case examples with accompanying clinical histories and 25 plotted T-JTA Profiles (in color).

The T-JTA Report Booklet is an eight-page booklet designed for use by the respondent to help them understand their T-JTA results. It is intended to emphasize what they learned during the interpretation and reinforce areas of strength and areas where attention may be needed.

The T-JTA can be scored by hand using Scoring Stencils or scored using computer software that are designed to save the counselor time and ensure scoring accuracy. Computer scoring results include *Profiling*, and optional *Brief* or *Interpretive Reports* with nine supplemental scales. A sample report can be viewed on their distributor's Web site at http://www.pearsonassessments.com/reports/f10csi.htm. Information is also available on the publisher's Web site at www.tjta.com (Taylor-Johnson Temperament Analysis® and T-JTA® are registered trademarks of Psychological Publications, Inc.).

PREP-M

This instrument was developed by Holman, Busby, and Larson. It is a 206-item survey, assessing five areas of readiness and background factors completed by individuals (in class or counseling settings), scored electronically, and used as a guide to discuss relationship strengths and work areas. It is actively being used as a research instrument. Original validation studies indicate that the norm population group consists of young Mormon couples at University. I am not aware if the instrument is used in common practice in Mormon premarital counseling. For more information, contact: The Marriage Consortium, 1000 SWKT, Brigham Young University, Provo, UT 84602; (802) 378-6419.

In my practice, I find the most valuable tool (and the most commonly used) is PREPARE/ENRICH. I highly recommend it. For couple's referred for a more thorough evaluation and after a standard evaluation, the 16PF can best be used to interpret both couple dynamics and generate an individual's clinical personality profile. I recommend this instrument for clinical evaluations. Pearson's Assessments offer two interpretative reports that are most appropriate for couple's counseling: the 16PF couples counseling report, and 16PF Karson Clinical Report, which yields more of a clinical personality profile (the profile does not meet DSM-IV criteria, but is useful in operationalizing personality dynamics). The same response sheet can be used to generate both reports.

FOCUS FOR CONTINUED PROFESSIONAL DEVELOPMENT

Freud wrote that it is the goal of therapy to help enable a patient to work and to love. Using marriage as a measure and in view of the high divorce rates, it seems that we therapists could do a better job.

Couples intending to marry for love believe that they can change the world. Most would agree that a healthy marriage and a growing family can change the world for the better in unimaginable ways.

To support that belief, psychologists try to intervene early and effectively. In other aspects of psychological practice, we've developed formal protocols for evaluations and feedback that are useful to the client or other interested parties. To date, no formal guidelines for protocol have been set by the licensing or ethical boards of psychologists or marriage and family therapists. Our state legislatures have written no mandate for counseling or the contents of such counseling. Seven states do encourage counseling, and Minnesota offers a $50 rebate off the cost of a marriage license for marital counseling.

Standardized guidelines would ensure a consistent and competent standard of care. Further research is indicated to describe the populations served by mental health professionals, develop a standardized protocol for premarital counseling in a mental health setting, and establish a referral network among professionals in other disciplines (clergypersons, attorneys, accountants, etc.).

There is also a need to continue the debate about mandatory prenuptial agreements and counseling for the benefit of all parties. Lacking a state mandate (which would take the pressure off the couple to propose such a thing), then professional organizations and licensing boards may consider writing their recommendations into standardized guidelines.

There is a great need to examine the educational curricula in graduate schools that prepare students for licensure as therapists to assure that techniques in premarital counseling are adequately addressed. Similarly, continuing education programs on the subject could improve therapists' comfort and competence in serving this population.

I have spoken with many fine therapists, skilled at working with individuals and groups, who do not feel comfortable working with couples. They've told me that working with couples can be more confusing than working in groups because there "is so much material to track." Each partner brings into the consulting room their well-established relationships with each other and their family-of-origin: their parents, siblings, and other relatives who were influential to them as they were growing up. When that happens, the room can get very crowded.

It can be daunting for a therapist to keep track of all the *transferences*, that is, all of the ways one relates to another *as if* they were someone else. At one moment, a couple can be relating to each other directly, as adults living in the present moment. At other times, an individual may become disorganized by certain emotional issues. He may then relate to his partner *as if* she were somebody else: his strict mother from childhood, his doting grandmother, etc. His responses, then, would be appropriate to that person attached to the transference, but not appropriate to his partner in the room.

Group therapists are familiar with *transferential relationships* that develop in groups of 5–9 members. In groups, members usually enter treatment after an introductory session with the therapist, but without introduction to their fellow group members. For example, candidates for a therapy group who are friends or relatives are rarely admitted into the same group, as this creates complicated alliances in the group and compromises confidentiality. It takes the group some time before familiarity and trust begins to grow. Likewise, it takes some time for transference-relationships to develop and be expressed in the treatment room. Therapists track these relationships as they develop and therefore may be more prepared, less "blind-sided," when such inappropriate exchanges are expressed. Hence, they may feel more comfortable working with the transference by facilitating the group interaction or by making appropriate interpretations.

Couples therapy differs from group in that the relationship between partners is well-developed before beginning treatment. Their transferential relationships with each other may have already developed and matured. Those relationships can be complex and based on their individual personalities and on the roles they assume for each other as spouses. Therefore, the transferences seem more focused, more intense, and more immediate. Therapists who are unprepared for such intense interactions, often beginning in the very first session, may feel overwhelmed and withdraw from treatment by ethically observing for the couple that their treatment is beyond the therapist's scope of practice and making an appropriate referral.

Given the large population of couples needing assistance with marital relationships, advanced training in couples dynamics could be offered to therapists at all levels of licensure in order to meet the need of the population and to improve our standard of care.

Bibliography

Barger, R. N. (1998). Summary of Lawrence Kohlberg's stages of moral development. Notre Dame, IN: University of Notre Dame, http://www.nd.edu/~rbarger/kohlberg.html

Barger, R. N., Kubitschek, W. N., & Barger, J. C. (April 13–17, 1998). Do philosophical tendencies correlate with personality types? A paper presented at the Annual Meeting of the American Educational Research Association, San Diego, CA.

Benjamin, G. A. H., & Gollan, J. (2003). *Family evaluation in custody litigation: Reducing risks of ethical infractions and malpractice* (Forensic Practice Guidebook), 1st ed. Washington, DC: American Psychological Association (APA).

Berrick, J. D., & Barth, R. P. (1992). Child sexual abuse prevention: Research review and recommendations. *Social Work Research and Abstracts*, 28, 6–15.

Bishop Pivarunas, Mark A. (October 7, 1997). Annulments in the Conciliar Church. Feast of the Holy Rosary. *CMRI*. http://www.cmri.org/97prog9-1.htm

Bowlby, J. (1979). *The making and breaking of affectional bonds*. London: Tavistock.

———. (1988). *A secure base: Clinical applications of attachment theory*. London: Routledge.

Bradbury, T. N., & Fincham, F. D. (1987). Affect and cognition in close relationships: Toward an integrative model. *Cognition and Emotion*, 1, 59–87.

Bramlett, M. D., & Mosher, W. D. (2001). *First marriage dissolution, divorce and remarriage: United States*. DHHS publication, no. (PHS) 2001-1250. Hyattsville, MD: Department of Health and Human Services, Centers for Disease Control and Prevention, National Center for Health Statistics.

Byng-Hall, J. (1999). Family couple therapy: Toward greater security. In J. Cassidy & P. R. Shaver (eds.), *Handbook of attachment: Theory, research, and clinical applications* (pp. 625–645). New York: Guilford Press.

Califano Jr., J. A. (2005). *Inside: A public and private life*, new ed. New York: PublicAffairs.

Carnelley, K. B., & Janoff-Bulman, R. (1992). Optimism about love relationships: General vs. specific lessons from one's personal experiences. *Journal of Social and Personal Relationships*, 9, 5–20.

Carrere, S., Buehlman, K., Gottman, J., Coan, J., & Ruckstuhl, L. (2000). Predicting marital stability and divorce in newlywed couples. *Journal of Family Psychology*, 14(1), 42–58.

Carroll, J. S., & Doherty, W. J. (2003). Evaluating the effectiveness of premarital prevention programs: A meta-analytic review of outcome research. *Family Relations*, 52(2), 105–118.

Chapman, Gary D. (September 2003). *Covenant marriage: Building communication & intimacy*. Broadman & Holman Publishers.

Dubin, Arlene. (2001). *Prenups for lovers: A romantic guide to prenuptial agreements*, 1st ed. New York: Villard.

Fincham, F. D., Bradbury, T. N., & Scott, C. K. (1990). Cognition in marriage. In F. D. Fincham & T. N. Bradbury (eds.), *The psychology of marriage* (pp. 118–149). New York: Guilford Press.

Fitzpatrick, C. (1995). Review of the PREPARE/ENRICH. In B. S. Plake, J. C. Impara, & R. A. Spies (eds.), *The fourteenth mental measurements yearbook* [Electronic version]. Retrieved February 17, 2006, from the Buros Institute's *Test Reviews Online* website: http://www.unl.edu/buros

Fonagy, P. (1999). Male perpetrators of violence against women: An attachment theory perspective. *Journal of Applied Psychoanalytic Studies*, 1, 7–27.

Fowers, B. J., Montel, K. H., & Olson, D. H. (1996). Predicting marital success based on couple types. *Journal of Marital & Family Therapy*, 22(1), 103–111.

Fowers, B.J., & Olson, D.H. (1992). Four types of premarital relationships: An empirical typology based on PREPARE. *Journal of Family Psychology*, 6, 10–21

The Future Foundation (August 2006). Calpol (1995). The changing face of parenting: Professional parenting, information and healthcare.

Giarretto, H. (1978). Humanistic treatment of father–daughter incest. *Journal of Humanistic Psychology*, 18, 59–76.

Goldstein, S., & Thau, S. (Published online: February 2, 2006). Attachment theory, neuroscience, and couple therapy. *International Journal of Applied Psychoanalytic Studies*, 1(3), 214–223.

Gottman, J. M. (1993). A theory of marital dissolution and stability. *Journal of Family Psychology*, 7, 57–75.

———. (1994). *What predicts divorce?: The relationship between marital processes and marital outcomes*. Hillsdale, NJ: Erlbaum.

Gottman, J. M., & Levenson, R. W. (2000). The timing of divorce: Predicting when a couple will divorce over a 14-year period. *Journal of Marriage & the Family*, 62, 737–745.

Haugaard, J., & Samwel, C. (1992). Legal and therapeutic interventions with incestuous families. *International Journal of Medicine and the Law*, 11, 469–484.

Holman, Thomas B. (November 2000). *Premarital prediction of marital quality or breakup—Research, theory, and practice* (Longitudinal Research in the Social and Behavioral Sciences: An Interdisciplinary Series), 1st ed. New York: Kluwer Academic/Plenum Publishers.

Huston, T., Caughlin, J., Houts, R., Smith, S., & George, L. (2000). How does personality matter in marriage? An examination of trait anxiety, interpersonal negativity, and marital satisfaction. *The Journal of Personality and Social Psychology*, 80, 237–252.

Kaplan, H. I., & Sadock, B. J. (2007). *Synopsis of psychiatry*, 10th ed. Baltimore: Williams & Wilkins.

Kliman, G., & Rosenfeld, A. (January 1, 1980). *Responsible parenthood: The child's psyche through the six-year pregnancy*, 1st ed. New York: Holt, Rinehart and Winston.

Kohlberg, L. A., Turner, M. E., Pratkanis, A. R. & Hardaway, T. J. (1991). Moral development inventory. *Journal of Social Behavior and Personality*, 6, 797–814.

Lewis, T., Amini, F., & Lannon, R. (2002). *A general theory of love*. New York: Vintage Press.

Mikulincer, M., Florian, V., Cowan, P., & Cowan, C. (Fall 2002). Attachment security in couple relationships: A systemic model and its implications for family dynamics. *Family Process*, 41 405–434.

Olsen, J. L., & Widom, C. S. (1993). Prevention of child abuse and neglect. *Applied and Preventive Psychology*, 2, 217–229.

Olson, D. H., & Knutson, L. (2003). Effectiveness of PREPARE program with premarital couples in community settings. *Marriage & Family: A Christian Journal*, 6(4), 529–546.

Once Were Warriors (1995). New Line Home Video ASIN: B0000A02Y4 MPAA: for pervasive language and strong depiction of domestic abuse, including sexual violence and substance abuse.

Parisi, F. *Spontaneous emergence of law: Customary law*. George Mason University School of Law.

Parisi, F. (2000). "Spontaneous Emergence of Law: Customary Law," in *Encyclopedia of Law and Economics*, vol. 5, pp. 603–630. Cheltenham, U.K.: Edward Elgar Publishing.

Piaget, J. (1962). The role of imitation in the development of representational thought. In H.E. Gruber & J. J. Voneche (eds.), *The Essential Piaget*. New York: Basic Books.

Pietromonaco, P., & Carnelley, K. (1994). Gender and working models of attachment: Consequences for perceptions of self and romantic partners. *Personal Relationships*, 1, 63–82.

Raley, R. K., & Bumpass, L. (April 2003). The topography of the divorce plateau: Levels and trends in union stability in the United States after 1980. *Demographic Research*, 8 (Article 8), 245–260.

Reppucci, N. D., & Haugaard, J. J. (1989). The prevention of child sexual abuse: Myth or reality? *American Psychologist*, 44, 1266–1275.

Robinson, E. A., & Price, M. G. (1980). Pleasurable behavior in marital interaction: An observational study. *Journal of Consulting and Clinical Psychology*, 48(1), 117–118.

Rose, D., Gonin, R., & Sammon, R. (1998). *Journal of the Royal Statistical Society: Series A (Statistics in Society)*, 161(3), 399–400.

Rudd, J. M., & Herzberger, S. D. (1999). Brother-sister incest–father-daughter incest: A comparison on of characteristics and consequences. *Child Abuse & Neglect*, 9, 915–928.

Russell, D. (1983). The incidence and prevalence of intrafamilial and extrafamilial sexual abuse of female children. *Child Abuse & Neglect*, 7, 133–146.

Sedlak, A. J., & Broadhurst, D. D. (1996). *Third national incidence study of child abuse and neglect*. Washington, DC: U.S. Department of Health and Human Services.

Shanhong, L., & Klohnen, E. (2005). Assortative mating and marital quality in newlyweds: A couple-centered approach. *Journal of Personality and Social Psychology*, 88, 237–252.

Siegel, J. M., Sorenson, S. G., Golding, J. M., Burnam, M., & Stein, J. (1987). The prevalence of childhood sexual abuse. *American Journal of Epidemiology*, 126, 1141–1153.

Smith, M. (2005). Letters and Arts, Inc. WeddingClipart.com, Ashland, Oregon.

Stahmann, R., & Hiebert, W. (1997). *Premarital & remarital counseling: The professional's handbook*. San Francisco, CA: Jossey-Bass.

Tatkin, S. (2003). A developmental psychobiological approach to couple therapy. In Allan N. Schore (ed.), *Psychoanalytic research: Progress and process notes from allan schore's groups in developmental affective neuroscience and clinical practice*. http://www.psybc.com/pdfs/library/Neurobiology_Attachment_CouplesTherapy1.pdf.

U.S. Department of Health and Human Services. (1999). Child maltreatment 1997: Reports from the states to the National Child Abuse and Neglect Data System. Washington, DC: U.S. Government Printing Office.

Warshak, Richard A. (March 1, 2003). *Divorce poison: Protecting the parent–child bond from a vindictive ex*. New York: Regan Books.

Weiss, R. L. (1980). Strategic behavioral marital therapy: Toward a model for assessment and intervention. In J. P. Vincent (ed.), *Advances in family intervention, assessment and theory* (Vol. 1, pp. 229–271). Greenwich, CT: JAI Press.

Whitaker, D. J., Beach, S. R. H., Etherton, J., Wakefield, R., & Anderson, P. L. (1999). Attachment and expectations about future relationships: Moderation by accessibility. *Personal Relationships*, 6, 41–56.

Wyatt, G. E. (1985). The sexual abuse of Afro-American and White-American women in childhood. *Child Abuse and Neglect*, 9, 507–519.

Zwach, J. P. (1983). *Annulment: Your chance to remarry within the Catholic Church*: A step-by-step guide using the new code of canon law, 1st ed. San Francisco: HarperSan Francisco.

Index

About the Author

JIM BIERMAN is a Licensed Clinical Psychologist with 12 years of experience in treating children, adults, couples, and families. In private practice now in Rancho Mirage, California, Dr. Bierman has also practiced in institutional and community settings in Seattle, London, Los Angeles, and rural northern California. Dr. Bierman is a Certified Parent Evaluator who evaluates parents in high-conflict child-custody cases and makes recommendations to the Court for residential placement of children. He received his Ph.D. from the California Graduate Institute and his postdoctoral training at the University of Washington School of Medicine Parent Evaluation Training Program.